# The Philosophy of Logical Atomism

## Bertrand Russell

Edited and with an introduction by

### David Pears

*Professor of Philosophy*
*University of Oxford*

*Metaphys*
*semantics*
*Epis*

*Error p. 90*

*Ord thgs as logical fictions 146*
*152*

### Open Court
Chicago and La Salle, Illinois

**To order books from Open Court,
call toll-free 1-800-815-2280.**

Fourth printing 1993
Fifth printing 1994
Sixth printing 1996
Seventh printing 1998

First published as 'The Philosophy of Logical Atomism,' 1918 and 'Logical Atomism,' 1924. These two works were published, with an introduction by David Pears, as *Russell's Logical Atomism* by Fontana Paperbacks, London, 1972. David Pears's new introduction to the Open Court edition was written in 1985 and is published for the first time here.

Printed and bound in the United States of America.

**Library of Congress Cataloging-in-Publication Data**

Russell, Bertrand, 1872–1970
    The philosophy of logical atomism.

    Previously published: Russell's Logical Atomism, 1972.
    Bibliography: p.
    Includes index.
    Contents: The philosophy of logical atomism (1918).—Logical atomism (1924).
    1. Logical atomism. 2. Meaning (Philosophy)
3. Wittgenstein, Ludwig, 1889–1951. 4. Proposition
(Logic) I. Pears, David Francis. II. Russell, Bertrand, 1872–1970.
Russell's logical atomism. III. Russell, Bertrand, 1872–1970.
Logical atomism.
1985. IV. Title.

BC199.L6R87    1985    146'.5    84-18750
ISBN 0-87548-443-3

# Contents

# Introduction

The best way to understand a philosophical theory is nearly always to try to appreciate the force of the arguments for it. Logical atomism is no exception. It is a theory about the fundamental structure of reality and so it belongs to the main tradition of western metaphysics. Its central claim is that everything that we ever experience can be analyzed into logical atoms. This sounds like physics but in fact it is metaphysics.

In *The Philosophy of Logical Atomism,* given as a series of lectures in the winter of 1917-18 and republished in this volume,[1] Russell says that his reason for calling his doctrine *logical* atomism is because:

> the atoms that I wish to arrive at as the sort of last residue in analysis are logical atoms and not physical atoms. Some of them will be what I call 'particulars'—such things as little patches of colour or sounds, momentary things—and some of them will be predicates or relations and so on. The point is that the atom I wish to arrive at is the atom of logical analysis, not the atom of physical analysis.[2]

His negative point is clear enough: they are not physical atoms. Their positive characterization is not so obvious. What exactly are logical atoms? He tells us that they are particulars, qualities, and relations, and he is evidently

---

[1]They were first published in *The Monist,* 1918, and reprinted in Russell: *Logic and Knowledge,* ed. R.C. Marsh, Allen & Unwin, London 1956.

[2]p. 37.

relying on the fact that, when we look at reality from a logical point of view, it seems to reduce to particular things possessing certain qualities and standing in certain relations to one another. At least, that is how we usually think and speak about it, and so that is how it has to be. If reality did not in fact fall apart in the way in which we carve it up in thought and speech, everything that we think and say about it would be radically mistaken.[3]

Here we have one of the premisses of Russell's logical atomism: there must be a general correspondence between the ways in which we divide up reality in thought and speech and the ways in which it divides up in fact.[4] It is an appealing premiss which at first sight may seem undeniable. But what if the realism is challenged? Can it really be justified? An idealist would point out that we can never verify the correspondence between thought and reality, because we can never apprehend reality as it is in itself, unaffected by the medium of thought.[5] Perhaps what really happens is that we project our categorizations onto the world. As Hume said, "The mind has a great propensity to spread itself on objects."[6]

Even if this premiss is conceded, it is not powerful enough on its own to support an argument for logical atomism. An atom is something indivisible or not further analyzable. A logical atomist, therefore, needs to show not only that the divisions traceable in logic correspond to real divisions in the nature of things, but also that the two corresponding processes of analysis do not continue indefinitely. If Russell is right, there must be a point at which words and things will be found to be not further analyzable. But why should we believe that?

---

[3]Cf. Plato: *Phaedrus* 265E, where an older analogy is used: philosophers should divide things at their natural joints as if they were dissecting sacrificial victims.

[4]This premiss is explicit in *Lecture VIII*.

[5]Cf. H. Putnam: *Realism and Reason: Philosophical Papers Vol. III*, Cambridge, 1983, Introduction.

[6]D. Hume: *A Treatise of Human Nature*, Book I, Part 3, §xiv.

In fact, he offers us more than one reason for believing it. In his later essay, *Logical Atomism,* published in 1924[7] and reissued in this volume, he says ". . .I confess it seems obvious to me (as it did to Leibniz) that what is complex must be composed of simples, though the number of constituents may be infinite."[8] This, of course, is an assertion rather than an argument, but it is quite a persuasive assertion. However, that may be only because it is a maxim useful for guiding our thoughts rather than a truth about the nature of things. That is how Kant thought of it.[9] But Russell certainly regarded it as a truth, albeit one that might never be established by the actual completion of a piece of logical analysis.

Much later, in 1959, defending his earlier ideas against J.O. Urmson's criticisms,[10] he said "As regards simples" (*i.e.* logical atoms) "I can see no reason either to assert or deny that they may be reached by analysis. Wittgenstein in the *Tractatus* and I on occasion spoke of 'atomic facts' as the final residue in analysis, but it was never an essential part of the analytical philosophy which Mr. Urmson is criticizing to suppose that such facts were attainable."[11]

Russell went on to defend this interpretation of his earlier philosophy by quoting from the discussion at the end of *Lecture II* : ". . .that is, of course, a question that might be argued—whether when a thing is complex it is necessary that it should in analysis have constituents that are simple. I think it is perfectly possible to suppose that complex things are capable of analysis *ad infinitum,* and that you never reach the simple. I do not think it is true, but it is a thing that one might argue, certainly."[12]

---

[7]*'Contemporary British Philosophy'* ed. J.H. Muirhead, London 1924. The essay was first republished in Russell: *Logic and Knowledge.*

[8]p. 173.

[9]*Critique of Pure Reason,* Transcendental Dialectic, Book II, Ch. 2, §ii.

[10]*Philosophical Analysis: its Development between the Two World Wars,* J.O. Urmson, Oxford 1956.

[11]*My Philosophical Development,* London 1959, p. 221.

[12]*The Philosophy of Logical Atomism,* p. 64.

Evidently there is some confusion in his recollection of his own earlier ideas. Given the general correspondence between language and reality, there were two views that he might have taken of logical atomism. One was that it had been verified by the actual completion of logical analysis. The other view was that it was self-evident, and so, even if nobody had yet verified it by completing any logical analysis, there could be no doubt of its truth. The first of these two views goes very well with the empiricism that he took over from Hume, while the second one, which he attributes to Leibniz, is more in keeping with rationalism. The view canvassed in the discussion at the end of *Lecture II* is quite different from both. It is really the negation of logical atomism and he mentions it in the discussion only to point out that it is not his view. So he ought not to have cited it later as evidence that he had approached logical atomism in the second, rationalist way. He did in fact use that approach, but what he said in the discussion at the end of *Lecture II* cannot be taken as evidence of that fact.

It may be useful to introduce names for the three views that have just been distinguished from one another. The two main lines of thought start from the assumption that there is a general correspondence between language and reality, which ensures that the complete analysis of words will match the complete analysis of things. One of them may be called 'The Empirical Approach' and the other 'The Rationalist Approach.'

The difference between them is not a difference of opinion about the nature of things, but only about the way to establish what their nature is. Both hold that reality is composed of logical atoms which are not further analyzable. A philosopher who uses the Rationalist Approach will claim that this conclusion is self-evidently true, or, at least, that it can be established by *a priori* reasoning. The Empirical Approach, on the other hand, leads to the claim that it is established by actual logical analysis. The idea is that, when we analyze the words in our vocabulary, we soon reach a point at which we find that we cannot analyze them any further, and so we conclude that we have reached the bottom line where unanalyzable words correspond to unanalyzable things.

The two views may be combined without any incoherence. They share the same conclusion, logical atomism, and they both incorporate the assumption of a general correspondence between language and reality. They differ only in their methods of establishing the conclusion. According to one view, it is established empirically, like the conjecture that every even number is the sum of two prime numbers, while the other view takes it to be provable, as it is hoped that the arithmetical conjecture will be proved one day. So Russell was not wrong when he allowed both views to be represented in his treatment of logical atomism.

However, their combination can produce a certain tension. For suppose that we are developing the empirical argument for logical atomism. How are we to know that the words which we cannot analyze any further really are not further analyzable? Is there not a danger that we may think we have reached the bottom line before we have really done so? Perhaps our 'logical atoms' are not really logical atoms at all, but only a stage on the way to a complete analysis.

At this point it is possible for a divergence to open up between the two approaches, because the difference between their methods of argument may lead to a difference between their conclusions about the nature of things. In fact, this is what happened to Russell and Wittgenstein. Russell used the empirical argument and claimed, in the spirit of Hume, that, when we find that we cannot push the analysis of words any further, we can plant a flag recording the discovery of genuine logical atoms. Wittgenstein disagreed, because he did not think that the actual progress of logical analysis to date yielded such a reliable indication. So he used an *a priori* argument instead and identified logical atoms outside the area explored by Russell.

The trouble was that, when Russell used the empirical

argument, the result was going to depend on whether he would make a premature identification of logical atoms, like Columbus in the Caribbean. Columbus believed that he had sailed far enough to reach India and Russell believed that he had taken the analysis of language far enough to reach logical atoms. Wittgenstein, on the other hand, did not rely on the results of logical analysis and used an *a priori* argument instead. So the two philosophers located the object of their search in different places.

When we look at the matter in this way, it may be possible to explain how Russell became confused in his recollection of his own earlier ideas. What he says at the end of *Lecture II* is that reality may not after all be composed of logical atoms, and so, given the assumption of general correspondence between language and reality, words too may be interminably analyzable. However, this third view, which may be called 'The No Terminus Theory' is very speculative and so, quite naturally, it produces a pragmatic reaction. If, in fact, we soon reach a point where we, at least, cannot push analysis any further, why not treat that as the bottom line? Why not forget about the endless analyzability of reality and identify logical atoms at the point at which logical analysis ends for us?

This pragmatic line leads to a considerable weakening of the assumption of general correspondence between language and reality. The correspondence would be perfectly preserved by an endless analysis of language, but the brief analysis with which we would have to content ourselves would not preserve it perfectly. Our logical atoms would not be ultimate because there would not be any ultimate logical atoms. Incidentally, this No Terminus Theory comes very close to abandoning realism. Logical atoms become a kind of projection of the only analysis that we find ourselves able to achieve.

It is possible that this pragmatic line of thought explains the confusion in Russell's later recollections. For it is really only a more extreme development of the Empirical Approach. In fact, there is some evidence that Russell looked at the matter in this way in 1924. Just before the passage already quoted from *Logical Atomism* he writes:

> When I speak of 'simples', I ought to explain that I am speaking of something not experienced as such, but known only inferentially as the limit of analysis. It is quite possible that, by greater logical skill, the need for assuming them could be avoided. A logical language will not lead to error if its simple symbols (*i.e.* those not having any parts that are symbols, or any significant structure) all stand for objects of some one type, even if these objects are not simple. The only drawback to such a language is that it is incapable of dealing with anything simpler than the objects which it represents by simple symbols.[13]

This is cautious rationalism associated with tentative pragmatism. The *a priori* argument for ultimate logical atoms is not completely endorsed and the suggestion is almost made that there are two degrees of simplicity or atomicity. There are things that are simple for us, and there are, or may be, things that are really simple.

Be that as it may, the two main lines of thought, which must be kept in mind by anyone trying to understand Russell's logical atomism, are the Empirical Approach and the Rationalist Approach. The former is dominant in *The Philosophy of Logical Atomism* and so it may be worked out in detail first, and the recessive Rationalist Approach, preferred by Wittgenstein, may be left for later treatment. That is the plan to be followed in the remainder of this Introduction.

When Russell applied his newly developed logic to metaphysics and the theory of knowledge, his main ambition was to rebuild empiricism on firmer foundations. Previous empiricists, from Hume to J.S. Mill, had relied on a theory of mind which stood on the shifting sands between philosophy and psychology. Russell wished to replace this

---

[13]p. 173.

theory with something more robust. His new theory would be concerned with the expression of thoughts rather than with their psychological structure, and so would make everything open to view and amenable to scientific treatment. It would be a new theory of language rigorously constructed on the framework provided by the new logic.[14]

We are by now accustomed to this innovation. One way to appreciate its originality at the time is to contrast Russell's empiricism with Hume's. In his *Enquiry Concerning Human Understanding* Hume wrote:

> Complex ideas may, perhaps, be well known by definition, which is nothing but an enumeration of those parts or simple ideas, that compose them. But when we have pushed up definitions to the most simple ideas, and find still some ambiguity and obscurity; what resource are we then possessed of? By what invention can we throw light on these ideas, and render them altogether precise and determinate to our intellectual view? Produce the impressions or original sentiments, from which the ideas are copied.

He then went on to compare this method with the invention of "a new microscope or species of optics."[15]

Russell's logical version of empiricism differs from this psychological version in many ways. Instead of dealing with complex ideas, he deals with complex symbols or words. Words do not copy things but designate them, and so designation replaces the replication, which in Hume's system links ideas to impressions. But underneath these differences there are important structural similarities between the two versions of empiricism. Hume uses definitions to resolve complex ideas into their elements and Russell uses them to resolve complex symbols into theirs.

---

[14]See *The Philosophy of Logical Atomism* pp. 58-59. Cf. *Our Knowledge of the External World as a Field for Scientific Method in Philosophy*, pp. 49-69. The first of these two passages explains the relation between a logical language and ordinary language, and the second contains the main message of a chapter entitled *Logic as the Essence of Philosophy*.

[15]*Enquiry Concerning Human Understanding*, §VII pt. i.

When no further analysis is possible because the ideas or symbols are indefinable, Hume has recourse to impressions, the original input of the mind, and Russell has recourse to acquaintance, the basic relation between the mind and its objects.[16]

Hume and Russell both use the empirical argument for atomism: when we analyze ideas or words, we soon find that we cannot proceed any further, because definition, the tool of analysis, can do no more. When this happens, we know that we have reached the bottom line: psychological atoms in Hume's theory, logical atoms in Russell's. This is a clear example of the use of an empirical method in philosophy. What Russell hoped was that the method would be more perspicuous and would lead to firmer results if it were applied to language rather than to thought.[17] This never occurred to Hume, who claimed that his kind of examination of ideas was the "new species of optics."

There are two distinct reasons why this method goes very well with empiricism. One is that it brings philosophy down to earth by substituting empirical investigation for *a priori* argument. The other is that it is natural to use this philosophical method, as Russell did, to put empiricism itself, a particular philosophical doctrine, on a sound basis. So when analysis could proceed no further, he appealed to acquaintance or direct experience. It is important not to confuse these two reasons with one another. Empiricism is a philosophical theory about the sources and limits of human knowledge, and, though it goes very well with the use of an empirical method in philosophy, there is no necessary connection between the two.

Russellian analyses proceed by way of definitions, terminate with indefinables, and, at that point, base themselves on acquaintance. His procedure is fairly easy to

---

[16]See D.F. Pears: *Hume's Empiricism and Modern Empiricism,* in *David Hume, a Symposium,* ed. D.F. Pears, London 1963, reprinted as Ch. 7 of D.F. Pears: *Questions in the Philosophy of Mind,* London 1975.

[17]See Russell: *Our Knowledge of the External World,* loc. cit.

follow when he is analyzing general words, but his extension of the same kind of analysis to singular words or
expressions leads to notorious difficulties. It is, therefore,
best to start with his analysis of general words.

A hexagon is, by definition, a plane figure with six
straight sides. Someone who had never seen one could
learn the meaning of the word 'hexagon' through its definition, provided that he had seen other kinds of plane figures
with straight sides and could count. He would not need to
be acquainted with hexagons themselves, so long as he was
acquainted with the elements required for the definition of
the word. So far, this is close to Hume's account of the
composition of complex ideas and of the two ways in
which we can acquire them: either we can build them up
out of their elements, or else we can get the corresponding
complex impressions. Russell's account is, of course, overtly
linguistic, whereas Hume's was psychological in spite of his
explicit use of definitions in the analysis of complex ideas.[18]
But the similarity is close.

There is, however, an important new development in
Russell's treatment of the topic. The function of definitions
in his theory is to allow us to learn the meanings of complex words without acquaintance with the things designated by them. But the definition of a complex word may
be perfectly correct without being the kind of definition
that can perform this function. For example, he points out
that colours can be defined by their wavelengths, but that
kind of definition would not put us in a position to recognize without the use of scientific instruments colours that
we had not previously seen.[19] So it would be quite unlike
defining a hexagon as a plane figure with six straight sides.
The difference is that the definition of a colour by its
wave-length does not epitomize the way in which we actually apply the colour-word, but the definition of a hexagon

---

[18]See *Enquiry Concerning Human Understanding,* loc. cit.
[19]See *The Philosophy of Logical Atomism,* pp. 53-55.

does do that. So Russell distinguished between the two kinds of definition. Those that epitomize the application of words and put us in a position to recognize in the ordinary way things that we have not previously seen are analyses and the others are not analyses.

To put the point in another way, a Russellian analysis of a word always follows a route which traces a possible way of learning its meaning. Each bifurcation marks a point at which it would be possible to stop and achieve the acquaintance that would impart the meaning of the word. If, for some reason, acquaintance is not available at that point, the would-be learner has to continue the analysis. Since Russellian acquaintance is direct experience, this theory of analysis is a straightforward version of empiricism. This comes out very clearly in his treatment of simple qualities and relations. In their case, there are no bifurcations and no further analysis is possible, and the need for acquaintance must be met immediately, because there is nowhere else to go.

Russell gives determinate shades of colour as examples of simple qualities, just as Hume had done before him.[20] The fact that the word 'scarlet' can be defined by the wave-length of the colour is no help to the would-be learner, or at least not help of the right kind, and so he has to achieve acquaintance with the colour itself. This important doctrine may be called 'The Theory of Forced Acquaintance.' If a would-be learner of the meaning of a word designating a quality is forced to achieve acquaintance with the quality itself, that indicates that it is a simple quality.[21] Here we have Russell's dominant criterion of atomicity: the quality is a logical atom, because it is a logical atom for us. Naturally, when he proposes this criterion, his suspicion, that the possibility of logical analysis might extend further than we are now able to exploit it, is recessive. It

---

[20] D. Hume: *A Treatise of Human Nature*, Book I, Pt 1, § i.
[21] *The Philosophy of Logical Atomism ibid.*

is really striking how close his dominant empirical criterion is to Hume's criterion: a simple idea, according to Hume, is one that can only be derived from the corresponding impression.

Up to this point, though many of Russell's doctrines are questionable, their meaning and interconnections are tolerably clear. However, his extension of the same doctrines to singular expressions and the particulars designated by them is much more difficult to understand. But before we go into those problems, it might be useful to review the main doubts felt by other philosophers about the doctrines already expounded.

One doubt, mentioned earlier, is whether the general framework of Russell's realism is acceptable. Perhaps it is only a projection of our own habits of thought. There are also several points at which his theory of meaning has been questioned. Is the ability to recognize a quality or relation quite so large a part of knowing the meaning of the word designating it? A better alternative might be to think of a word as a single knot in a net. Then it would be the whole net that captured reality, and the meanings of single words would be given by their positions in the net rather than by their separate connections with the things that they designated. Wittgenstein put this point by saying that the meaning of a word is given by its role in a language-game.[22] Atomism is the exact opposite of this kind of holism.

Even if Russell's atomism were generally acceptable, there are difficulties in his account of the learning of meanings. Is it really true that the ability to recognize a determinate shade of colour can be acquired only through acquaintance with the colour itself? Hume's remarks about a shade of blue not represented in his experience are enough to raise a reasonable doubt on this point.[23] Finally,

---

[22]See *Philosophical Investigations,* passim.

[23]They occur at the end of *A Treatise of Human Nature* Book I, Pt 1, § i. Professor H.A. Prichard in his lectures on Hume at Oxford used to call Hume's refusal to modify his theory of simple qualities in the light of these counter-examples "brazen effrontery."

Russell's treatment of essence might be questioned. As an empiricist he was preoccupied with learning the meanings of words by actual confrontation with the things designated by them and this led him to identify the essences of things with their accepted recognitional properties. But the advances of science since the Renaissance have made that identification very questionable. For example, Putnam has argued that the essence of a disease is its viral or bacterial causation rather than the clinical symptoms by which it is recognized, because the symptoms can vary over time without any change in the underlying identity of the disease.[24]

When Russell extended his theory of logical analysis to singular expressions, he encountered a number of further difficulties. The apparatus of Humean empiricism had to be adjusted to fit the logic of proper names and definite descriptions like 'The King of France.' The logic of these expressions depended on a lot of very subtle considerations, some of which had been explored by J.S. Mill[25] and G. Frege,[26] but there was no general agreement about the weight to be attached to them in a well-balanced theory. Proper names obviously do designate particulars, but there was (and still is) a lot of controversy about the way in which they do it and about the knowledge that is required for their effective use. Russell's view was that ordinary proper names are complex expressions which can therefore be analyzed. However, he also believed that there must be unanalyzable proper names which make the same kind of pinpoint contact with simple particulars that unanalyzable adjectives make with simple qualities.

---

[24]E.g. the plague in Athens at the end of the 5th century B.C. was probably measles. See H. Putnam: *Dreaming and 'Depth Grammar'*, especially pp. 310-15 of *Philosophical Papers, Vol. II*, Cambridge, 1975, where this article is reprinted. Cf. H. Putnam: *The Meaning of 'Meaning'*, especially pp. 245-257 of the same volume.

[25]See J.S. Mill: *A System of Logic*, Book I Ch. 1 § 5.

[26]See G. Frege: *Sense and Reference* in *Translations from the Philosophical Writings of Gottleb Frege*, Peter Geach and Max Black, Oxford 1966.

So there are two layers of difficulties here. First, there are the basic problems about the logic of singular expressions. Second, on top of these problems which are inherent in the subject, there are special problems about Russell's distinction between ordinary, analyzable proper names and unanalyzable proper names. For the parallelism between his analysis of general expressions and his analysis of singular expressions is hard to establish in detail and it is not clear exactly how he saw it. Interpretation has to start from the contrast between ordinary proper names, like London, and the unanalyzable proper names which he thought that his theory required, and which he called "logically proper names."[27]

According to him, ordinary proper names are analyzable as definite descriptions: London is the capital of Britain, the largest port on the River Thames, etc. There are notorious difficulties about the choice of a particular definite description to serve as the analysis of an ordinary proper name, but the point to notice first about these descriptions is that they do not seem to divide the thing into its elements. In the example given they are just the ordinary kind of description that would help a tourist to identify the city, and Russell always uses examples of this kind in *The Philosophy of Logical Atomism*. It might be thought that this is because it was given as a set of popular lectures, but it will soon appear that there is more to it than that.

His view about logically proper names is that they cannot be analyzed in the same way as ordinary proper names or in any other way. They are, according to him, the names of particular sense-data: for example, '*n*' might be the name of the small patch of blue now in the centre of my visual field. At first sight, it is puzzling that he says that '*n*' is unanalyzable. Why should it not be analyzed by the definite description, 'The small patch of blue . . . etc.'? What difference did Russell see between the logically proper

---

[27] *The Philosophy of Logical Atomism*, pp. 61-63.

name, '$n$', and an ordinary proper name like 'London'? It is true that I could describe London by giving its internal structure, and perhaps it is true that I could not give that kind of description of a very small patch in my visual field. But that difference seems to be irrelevant, because Russell does not use that kind of description to analyze ordinary proper names. London is the capital of Britain, Aristotle the teacher of Alexander, and so on. Why then does he insist that logically proper names are unanalyzable?

One possible justification for singling out logically proper names for special treatment would be a certain kind of essentialism. The idea would be that some descriptions give the essential properties of things while others give their accidental properties. The mere fact that a sense-datum satisfied a certain description would not be enough to show that its name was analyzable. For the description might attribute an accidental property to it—it might just happen to be blue—and that would not indicate that its name was analyzable. It would be analyzable only if it satisfied a description attributing an essential property to it; if no such description could be found, it would be unanalyzable. So Russell needed a way of distinguishing essential properties of things from their accidental properties.

This is exactly what one would expect after reading his account of the analysis of general words. It is an essential property of hexagons that they should have six straight sides, but only an accidental property that they should be the shape preferred by bees when they are constructing their cells. Incidentally, if he did have a way of distinguishing the essential properties of things from their accidental properties, one of the problems produced by his analysis of ordinary proper names could be solved. The name 'Aristotle' would not be analysed by the definite description the teacher of Alexander, because it is only a contingent fact that Aristotle taught Alexander.[28] This kind of

---

[28]This point is developed by S. Kripke in *Naming and Necessity*, Oxford 1980, pp. 49-78.

analysis would work for an ordinary proper name only when the description attributed an essential property to the person or thing named by it. If the thing possessed no essential properties, its name would be unanalyzable, a logically proper name.

How then did Russell draw the distinction that he needed between the essential properties of particulars and their accidental properties? The answer is strangely disappointing. In the case of ordinary proper names he seems to have been unaware of the need to put any restriction on the kind of definite description used in their analysis. This cannot be discounted as a feature of a popular exposition, because it is not confined to *The Philosophy of Logical Atomism* but recurs in all his treatments of the topic. Like Frege, he allowed any description satisfied by a complex particular to serve as the analysis of its name.

It is true that essentialism is not the only way of imposing a restriction on definite descriptions acceptable as analyses. 'The author of the Iliad' and 'The man they are talking about at the next table'[29] are examples of accidental descriptions which may play a privileged role in introducing names. However, essentialism was clearly the best basis for the kind of restriction that Russell needed, because it selects definite descriptions in a way that does not depend on the context but always remains constant for a given particular. Surprisingly, he made no use of it or of any other method for achieving a restriction in the case of ordinary proper names.

However, his theory of logically proper names does rely on a rudimentary version of essentialism. It must do, because otherwise the mere fact that sense-data possess properties would be enough to show that they cannot be

---

[29]See S. Kripke, *loc. cit.,* pp. 57-9 on the use of an accidental description to fix the reference of a name. The second example illustrates what G. Evans calls 'the deferential use of a proper name': see *The Causal Theory of Names,* Proceedings of the Aristotelian Society, Supp. Vol. 1975, p. 205. But see also G. Evans *Varieties of Reference,* Oxford 1982, p. 387.

simple particulars. He must be assuming that sense-data are simple because they have no essential individuating properties, or, at least, no specifiable ones. He must, therefore, have been using some criterion to distinguish the essential from the accidental properties of particulars. What was it? It seems that he assumed that the essential properties of an individual, if it has any, will be features of its structure or composition. This is an assumption that a practitioner of logical analysis would hardly notice that he was making. It is part of the standard picture of analysis.

This interpretation is not entirely inferential, because there is direct evidence for it in the texts. For example, at the beginning of *Lecture III* he expatiates on the self-subsistence of simple particulars: ". . .each particular has its being independently of any other and does not depend upon anything else for the possibility of its existence." He then develops a comparison between his simple particulars and "the old conception of substance." His simple particulars possess

> the quality of self-subsistence that used to belong to substance, but not the quality of persistence through time. [*sc.* because they are short-lived sense-data.] A particular, as a rule, is apt to last for a very short time indeed, not an instant but a very short time. In that respect particulars differ from the old substances but in their logical position they do not.[30]

This passage, taken by itself, does not actually prove that what makes a Russellian particular simple is its lack of structure or composition. For compositeness is not the only impediment to logical independence or self-subsistence. One particular, $A$, might depend on another particular, $\alpha$, for the logical possibility of its existence, even though $\alpha$ was not a component of $A$. For example, $A$ might be a Rembrandt and $\alpha$ the painter himself. However, Russell's conception of logical analysis made him blind to the im-

---

[30]*The Philosophy of Logical Atomism*, p. 65.

portance of this kind of case. Analysis, as the word implies, is taking something to pieces, and so, if the essence of a thing is going to be revealed by the logical analysis of its name, it must be a feature of its structure or composition. Simplicity, therefore, is equivalent to lack of structure, or at least to lack of specifiable structure.

Russell's view of simple qualities, like scarlet, is similar but not quite the same. It would have been exactly the same if he had held that there are no logical connections between simple qualities. That was the line taken by Wittgenstein, who therefore concluded that shades of colour are not simple.[31] Russell's requirement for simple qualities was less demanding: there might be logical connections between them, but they must not be connections of a kind that would allow someone to learn the meaning of a colour-word without acquaintance with the colour itself.[32] In other words, he insisted only on the Doctrine of Forced Acquaintance. However, underneath this difference between his conception of the simplicity of particulars and his conception of the simplicity of qualities there is a striking similarity: simplicity is equivalent to lack of internal structure.

Russell never developed this version of essentialism in a systematic way and he never applied it to ordinary proper names. It is, as it were, an important part of the drama which never quite gets on to the stage—something outside the tragedy, as Aristotle says in *The Poetics*. However, though this essentialism remained rudimentary in his writings, his logical atomism cannot be understood without it. If he had not relied on a distinction between essential and accidental properties, his claim, that the logically proper names of sense-data cannot be analyzed as definite descriptions, would

---

[31]See *Tractatus Logico-Philosophicus*, 6.3751.

[32]In *Our Knowledge of the External World*, p. 62, Russell seems inclined to deny that there are any logical connections between atomic facts. However, the context shows that he is thinking of pairs like 'a is red' and 'b is green' rather than pairs like 'a is red' and 'a is green'.

be unintelligible. If I cannot analyze '*n*' as 'the small blue patch now in the centre of my visual field', there must be some reason why this analysis is inadmissible, and the same reason ought to explain why I cannot analyze 'scarlet' as 'the colour of geraniums.' The only reason that can  ⟵ plausibly be ascribed to Russell is structural essentialism.

The most direct evidence for this interpretation can be found in his essay, *The Relation of Sense-data to Physics*. It is commonly supposed that he regarded all sense-data as simple particulars. However, in an important but neglected passage in this essay he points out that some of them are complex particulars.[33] He gives as an example a sense-datum consisting of a patch of blue to the left of a patch of red. This is a complex sense-datum, because it has an internal structure and two distinguishable components. Wittgenstein used a similar example in his review of logical atomism in *Philosophical Investigations*[34]: the sentence, "The broom is in the corner" was supposed to be analyzed as "The brush is attached to the stick and they are both in the corner." Here the complex particular is a material object rather than a sense-datum but the point made about its structure is the same.

If we turn from Russell's theory of analysis to its application, the evidence for this interpretation becomes overwhelming. His main ambition was to analyze tables and chairs, cabbages and kings, as series of sense-data.[35] Any analysis of that kind would have two important peculiarities. First, unlike the example used by Wittgenstein, it would involve a shift of category. Second, as a consequence, it would be a branching analysis, moving from a single complex particular to a series of simple particulars. For sense-data are more short-lived than material objects and so the analysis of a material object will always require a very large number of them. The result will be quite

---

[33]*Mysticism and Logic*, pp. 145ff. See especially p. 147.
[34]*Philosophical Investigations*, § 60.
[35]See *The Philosophy of Logical Atomism*, pp. 50-51 and pp. 143-155.

unlike the analysis of 'Scott' as 'The author of Waverley'[36] or the analysis of 'Bismarck' as 'The ego which. . . .'.[37]

Russell pictured the analysis of a complex singular expression as a ramifying process which would terminate with the logically proper names of sense-data. The shift of category raises a number of notorious problems. Can each of us really name his own sense-data and describe them without depending in any way on the external world or other peoples' reactions? Wittgenstein gave a negative answer, arguing that the necessarily unteachable language required by this theory could not even be set up by a single person for his own private use.[38] Even if he could set it up, communication with anyone else would be impossible, because nobody could achieve the acquaintance with anyone else's sense-data that he would need to understand their statements about them. These are problems on the borderline between semantics and the theory of knowledge. There are also some difficult metaphysical questions about sense-data. Are they really self-subsistent? And what account can be given of sense-data that are not actual but only possible?

However, if we look at Russell's theory from a logical point of view, the most important question that has not yet been answered is about the link between a logically proper name and the simple particular designated by it. What is the nature of this link and how is it established?

Part of the answer is straightforward. Someone is confronted by a simple particular—in Russell's theory, he is acquainted with a simple sense-datum—and he gives it a logically proper name, 'n'. If he used 'n' again later to refer to the sense-datum—in Russell's theory, he would have to be relying on experience-memory and perhaps even on

---

[36]*Loc. cit.* pp. 109-112.

[37]This is a rare example of an analysis of a complex particular which is non-branching but involves a shift of category. See Russell: *Knowledge by Acquaintance and Knowledge by Description,* in *Mysticism and Logic,* p. 218.

[38]*Philosophical Investigations,* passim.

short-term experience-memory[39]—he would mean that very same sense-datum. To put the point in Kripke's way, '*n*' would be the rigid designator of that sense-datum, because in virtue of its meaning it would designate the same sense-datum in every possible world in which it existed.[40] Naturally, this does not imply that *n* exists necessarily, because it would be possible to plant the name on *n* in the actual world and then to speculate that in another possible world *n* might not have existed.

But why did Russell not extend the same treatment to ordinary proper names? Kripke's theory is that ordinary proper names are rigid designators: an infant was christened 'Richard Nixon' and thereafter that name rigidly designates that person. Why did Russell not anticipate this theory of ordinary proper names?

In fact, he does half anticipate it. For he sometimes says that ordinary proper names can be used as names rather than as covert definite descriptions, and, when he says this, he means that they can be used as logically proper names, which are, in fact, the rigid designators of simple particulars. There is a clear example in *Lecture VI:*

> I should like to make clear what I was saying just now, that if you substitute another name in place of 'Scott' which is also a name of the same individual, say, 'Scott is Sir Walter', then 'Scott' and 'Sir Walter' are being used as names and not as descriptions, your proposition is strictly a tautology.[41] If one asserts 'Scott is Sir Walter', the way one would mean it would be that one was using the names as descriptions. One would mean that the person called 'Scott' is the person called 'Sir Walter', and 'the person called "Scott"' is a description, and so is 'the person called "Sir Walter"'.

---

[39]See Russell: *On the Experience of Time,* Monist 1915 and *The Philosophy of Logical Atomism,* p. 65, which imply that acquaintance with particulars does not reach beyond the limit of the specious present.

[40]S. Kripke, *Naming and Necessity,* pp. 47-9.

[41]The meaning of this sentence is unmistakable, but it would have been more accurately expressed if Russell had inserted the word 'and' twice, once before "say" and again before "your."

So that would not be a tautology. It would mean that the person called 'Scott' is identical with the person called 'Sir Walter'. But if you are using both as names, the matter is quite different. . . .if I say 'Scott is Sir Walter', using these two names *as* names, neither 'Scott' nor 'Sir Walter' occurs in what I am asserting, but only the person who has these names, and thus what I am asserting is a pure tautology.[42]

This remarkable passage makes Kripke's point, that, when two rigid designators flank the identity-sign, the resulting statement is necessarily true, if it is true at all.[43] For in such a case the identity will hold in virtue of the meanings of the two rigid designators.

It might be thought that Russell's concession, that ordinary proper names may be used as logically proper names, is merely a feature of a series of popular lectures. In such a context it is natural for him to use material objects to introduce points that are really about sense-data, and so he warns his audience that in the sentence 'This is white' the word 'This' functions as a logically proper name only when it is used "quite strictly, to stand for an actual object of sense" rather than "for this piece of chalk as a physical object".[44] However, there is more to it than that. For even if we chose our examples exclusively from sense-data and substituted two names of a complex sense-datum for the two names of the man, 'Scott' and 'Sir Walter', his point about the use of ordinary proper names as logically proper names would still have a valid application: if two names of the same complex sense-datum were used as logically proper names, the resulting identity-statement would be 'a pure tautology'.

This is an important point, because it shows that Russell's logically proper names combine two different features which could easily come apart. A sense-datum does not have a specifiable individual essence and so its logically

---

[42]*The Philosophy of Logical Atomism*, p. 114.
[43]See *Naming and Necessity*, pp. 99-105 and pp. 143-4.
[44]*The Philosophy of Logical Atomism*, p. 62.

proper name is unanalyzable. That is the first feature of
Russellian logically proper names. Their second feature,
which follows from it given the Doctrine of Forced Acquaintance, is that they must be directly attached to the
sense-data that they designate without the mediation of
any essential description. Now Russell never drew the clear
line that he needed between essential and accidental descriptions. He therefore regarded direct attachment as attachment unmediated by any description whatsoever. So
according to him, when I use the logically proper name,
'n', it will designate this particular sense-datum, whatever
descriptions it satisfies, and what I say about it will be said
*de re*.[45]

However, these two features might well come apart.
For it would be possible to attach a name directly to a
complex sense-datum when one was acquainted with it. It
would not matter that this sense-datum satisfied both accidental and essential descriptions. For the attachment would
not be mediated by them, just as it was not mediated by
the accidental descriptions of the simple sense-datum in
the other case. Here too the name would be used to designate that particular sense-datum in *de re* statements. Or, to
revert to the kind of example that Russell employed to
make this point, an ordinary proper name might be directly attached to a person with exactly the same sequel.

It is worth looking more closely at what he says about
the second feature of his logically proper names: "We are
not acquainted with Socrates, and therefore cannot name
him. When we use the word 'Socrates', we are really using
a description. Our thought may be rendered by some such

---

[45]When Russell explains how the ego is known by description, it is important for him to be able to start from *de re* knowledge of sense-data. See
*On the Nature of Acquaintance* in *Logic and Knowledge*, p. 168: "The subject at-
tending to 'this' is called 'g'. . . . 'This' is the point from which the whole
process starts, and 'this' itself is not defined but simply given. The confusions
and difficulties arise from regarding 'this' as *defined by the fact of being given,*
rather than simply as given." His point is that if it were defined as given, it
would be defined as given to the ego, which would be circular.

phrase as 'The Master of Plato', . . . but we certainly do not use the name as a name in the proper sense of the word.''[46] His reason for saying this is not that Socrates belongs to the external world, but rather that he died long ago. It is, therefore, a little confusing to find him allowing that 'Scott' and 'Sir Walter' may be used as names "in the proper sense of the word". He should have made the point about his contemporaries.

The passage continues: "That makes it very difficult to get any instance of a name at all in the proper strict logical sense of the word. The only words one does use as names in the logical sense are words like 'this' or 'that'. One can use 'this' as a name to stand for a particular with which one is acquainted at the moment. We say 'This is white'. If you agree that 'This is white,' meaning the 'this' that you see, you are using 'this' as a proper name."

He then issues the warning, already quoted, about the difference between the piece of chalk and a sense-datum. Finally, he points out that " 'this' has a very odd property for a proper name, namely that it seldom means the same thing two moments running, and does not mean the same thing to the speaker and the hearer. It is an *ambiguous* proper name, but it is really a proper name all the same, and it is almost the only thing I can think of that is used properly and logically in the sense that I was talking of for a proper name."

This needs some explanation. Two features of logically proper names have been distinguished, their unanalyzability and their direct attachment to things. Russell, as has been explained, allowed that ordinary proper names sometimes possess the second of these two features, but, of course, never the first. Now direct attachment is really attachment unmediated by any essential description. But because Russell never explicitly distinguished between essential and accidental descriptions, he regarded direct at-

---

[46]*The Philosophy of Logical Atomism*, p. 62.

tachment as attachment unmediated by any description whatsoever. So a directly attached name will designate the same thing in every possible world in which that thing exists, whatever descriptions it satisfies.

In the passage just quoted he says that the only words in ordinary language that function like logically proper names are demonstratives. He says this because he is thinking of the other feature of logically proper names, unanalyzability. Obviously, ordinary proper names do not designate simple particulars and so they fail the test of unanalyzability. If he had waived that requirement, he could have allowed that ordinary proper names fulfil the role of logically proper names to perfection. There is no mystery about this. They would fulfil the role of logically proper names to perfection because that role would only be the direct attachment to things that is needed for *de re* statements.

However, he does not waive the requirement of unanalyzability. He, therefore, has to find in ordinary language singular expressions directly attached to simple sense-data. Now sense-data never recur, and so, of course, we do not feel any need to name them, and our nearest approach to naming them is picking them out by demonstratives. This is fairly close because a demonstrative really is directly attached to its sense-datum and it really does designate the same sense-datum in every possible world in which that sense-datum exists. However, unlike a name, it is not a rigid designator, because it does not perform this function solely in virtue of its meaning, but partly in virtue of the varying contexts of its use. So, judging it by the standard of a name, which it is not, Russell calls it 'ambiguous', which it is not.

The important thing is to understand how he gets himself into this position. He does so by asking too much of logically proper names. If he had insisted only on direct attachment to things, ordinary proper names would have passed muster too, and then the distinction between 'ordinary' and 'logically proper' would have collapsed. But he

requires something more of logically proper names, unanalyzability. However, at the same time, he shows his feeling
for the great semantic importance of direct attachment by
allowing that ordinary proper names may be used as logically proper names. The trouble is that once he has added
the second requirement, of unanalyzability, his failure to
find any perfect examples of logically proper names in
ordinary language is inevitable. We can use demonstratives directly attached to our sense-data, and, when we do
so, they designate the same sense-data in every possible
world in which those sense-data exist, but they do not
perform this function solely in virtue of their meanings. So
he is wrong to take the variations in what they designate
as a sign of ambiguity.

Russell's rehabilitation of empiricism relied on very
close cooperation between his semantics and his theory of
knowledge. It is, therefore, necessary to go a little more
deeply into the theory of acquaintance that supported his
theory of logically proper names. One important question
about Russellian acquaintance has already been raised.
How far does a person's acquaintance extend back into his
own past experience? To put the question in another way,
does it reach back any further than the limit of short-term
memory of the specious present? The point of the question
is that knowledge by description takes over where acquaintance peters out.

The answer is that Russell always allows acquaintance
with qualities and relations experienced in the more remote past, but he is less permissive about acquaintance
with particulars. For he was inclined to think that particulars move out of range of acquaintance when they move
out of the specious present. It is true that he did not reach
this conclusion in his first discussion of this topic,[47] but it
is firmly established in his mind by 1917.[48]

---

[47]See *The Problems of Philosophy*, pp. 114-8.
[48]See *The Philosophy of Logical Atomism*, p. 65.

It is an important conclusion, because, if acquaintance provides indispensable support for logically proper names, then any restriction imposed on the range of acquaintance will automatically restrict the situations in which logically proper names can be used and understood. Now this restriction will be imposed on logically proper names entirely because of the exigencies of their direct application to things. It would, therefore, remain in force even if logically proper names were not unanalyzable. Even if their direct application to things were not unavoidable, as it is in Russell's theory, but only one of two options—the other option being analysis into elements with which their users were acquainted—the restriction would still remain in force.

The reason for this is that Russell held that the direct application of a name to a complex particular also requires the support of acquaintance. To put the point in his way, acquaintance is needed when an ordinary proper name is used as a logically proper name. So if he had lived to read Kripke's treatment of ordinary proper names as rigid designators, his first reaction would certainly have been to insist on the support provided by acquaintance. But, given the restriction imposed by him on the range of acquaintance, this would have produced the following result: when someone applies an ordinary proper name to a particular with which he has had acquaintance in the past, it can be used as a logically proper name or rigid designator only if his acquaintance with it belongs to the specious present.

There are, however, objections to imposing this restriction on what Russell calls "the use of names as names", and one of the aims of recent work on proper names has been to remove it and to find alternative ways of supporting their use as rigid designators. A student of Russell's philosophy might well begin to develop the objections by criticizing his account of memory. It is implausible to suppose that, if I talk to someone called 'John' at a party, then, as the moment of the conversation recedes into the past, I am forced to use his name through the mediation of a definite description instead of using it as a name. What is needed here is some alternative kind of support for the continued use of his name as a name. A plausible candidate would be causation, specifically the kind of causation on which experience-memory depends.[49]

When we look at the history of the theory of proper names from this point of view, we can see recent causal theories as natural developments of an obvious criticism of the restriction of 'the use of a name as a name' which Russell based on his restriction of the range of acquaintance-memory. 'The use of a name as a name' must reach outside the field of the user's immediate awareness, beyond the limit of his short-term memory and across the boundaries separating his consciousness from other people's. Kripke deals with the last of these three extension of range by suggesting that proper names—in his view, rigid designators—may be supported by a causal line running back through the oral tradition to the original christening[50] and Evans argues for another version of the causal theory.[51]

There is a second question worth asking about Russell's theory of acquaintance. Did he really regard it as a kind of pinpoint contact with reality? If so, acquaintance would not involve any selection or interpretation. A person could be acquainted with a sense-datum without being acquainted with it as an instance of a specific type of thing, and he could be acquainted with one of its qualities without being acquainted with it as a determinate in a certain determinable range.

His definition of acquaintance in *On the Nature of Acquaintance*[52] and his informal treatment of it in *The Problems of Philosophy*,[53] both make it quite clear that this was his idea.

---

[49]See C.B. Martin and M. Deutscher: *The Causal Theory of Memory*, Philosophical Review, 1966.

[50]*Naming and Necessity*, pp. 91-7.

[51]*The Causal Theory of Names*, Proceedings of the Aristotelian Society Supplement, 1975.

[52]*Logic and Knowledge*, p. 162.

[53]Ch. V.

Acquaintance is a kind of knowledge and yet it is a purely extensional relation between subject and object. This is confirmed by his review of his theory of acquaintance in 1959, long after he had given it up. He explains that he no longer holds that sensations automatically give us knowledge when we have them, as the term 'sense-datum' implied: " 'Perception' as opposed to 'sensation' involves habit based upon past experience. We may distinguish sensation as that part of our total experience which is due to the stimulus alone, independently of past history. This is a theoretical core in the total occurrence. The total occurrence is always an interpretation in which the sensational core has accretions embodying habits."[54]

His criticism of his own earlier position is a just one. It is a criticism often made by Wittgenstein in his later writings, where it serves as the first step in his argument against the possibility of a private language. Certainly, it is very paradoxical to treat acquaintance as pinpoint contact. The problems inherent in this view can easily be seen in the case of qualities. When someone learns the meaning of a colour-word by being shown an object of that colour, he has to pick out the hue and ignore all the object's other features. Also, when he does pick it out, what really counts is not his momentary relationship with it, but its long-term effect: he should be able to recognize it next time he sees it. If we call this 'acquaintance' with the quality, then acquaintance will not be mere pinpoint contact. It will involve selection at the time and a recognitional capacity later.

The same is true of acquaintance with particulars. You do not claim acquaintance with a person simply on the ground that he has passed through your field of vision without your noticing him and without your acquiring the ability to recognize him next time. In Russell's theory this point is not so obvious as the parallel point about acquaint-

---

[54]*My Philosophical Development*, p. 143.

ance with qualities and relations. For his simple particulars
are sense-data and so, unlike people and comets, they do
not recur and there is no possibility of re-identifying them.
However, that does not altogether cancel the usual requirements for acquaintance. You must still pick out your sense-
datum, say as a particular member of the class of visual
sense-data, and, even if you are never going to have an
opportunity to re-identify it, you must know at the time
which one it is and later which one it was. So this kind of
acquaintance too is more than pinpoint contact. It has to
plant a name in the world.

The marriage arranged by Russell between logic and
empiricism gives *The Philosophy of Logical Atomism* its special
character. Most of his emphasis is on the empirical argument for logical atomism: if we think of a word and begin
to analyze it by substituting definitions, we soon reach a
point at which the supply of definitions runs out and the
analysis terminates. The empirical argument claims that
this shows that we have reached logical atoms.

We may ignore the No Terminus Theory which makes
a brief appearance at the end of *Lecture II,* because it is not
any kind of version of logical atomism. For though it em-
ploys the same analytical method, it maintains that it never
reaches any bottom line on which logical atoms might be
identified. The only importance of this theory in the development of Russell's philosophy is that it would imply that
our powers of analysis are necessarily deficient.

This implication becomes more interesting when it is
modified—our powers of analysis have not yet been developed as far as they might be—and when it is combined
with the Rationalist Approach, which treats logical atomism as self-evident or provable *a priori.* This combination,
as was pointed out earlier, does not necessarily lead to a
rejection of the assumption of a general correspondence
between language and reality. For a full analysis of language would still be as fine-grained as reality itself. However it might lead to a certain weakening of the assumption,

because it might seem to open up the possibility of distin-
guishing between absolute atomicity and atomicity
relativized to our present analytical achievements.

Wittgenstein was opposed to any such dilution of pure
atomicity, even if it was only part of a compromise allowing for two degrees of the property. So, if we want to see
the Rationalist Approach disentangled from Russell's empiricism and followed to its true end, we should look at the
early philosophy of Wittgenstein.

Wittgenstein did not take logical atomism to be self-
evident but tried to deduce it by an *a priori* argument from
his theory of language. He believed, like Russell, that an
ordinary descriptive sentence depends for its meaning on
the fact that at some point in its analysis there are words
actually standing for things. Now on the No Terminus
Theory all things would be complex. Therefore, at the
point where designation occurred, it would have to be
designation of complex things. But from this it follows that
at that point further sentences would have to be true. For
it would have to be true that the elements of those complex
things were put together in a way that was required for
their existence.

So, to pick up the beginning of the argument again, if
the analysis of ordinary descriptive sentences never termi-
nated on logical atoms, their meaning would always depend on further factual truths. But that would not be
acceptable, because it would make meaning indetermi-
nate. The meaning of any descriptive sentence would depend on a truth, whose meaning would depend on a further
truth, and so on *ad infinitum.*[55]

Russell probably became aware of this argument only
when he read the *Tractatus* just after the First World War.

---

[55]See *Tractatus* 2.0211-2.022 and 3.23-3.24. Cf. *Notes Dictated to G.E. Moore
in Norway* in *Notebooks 1914-16,* p. 116: "The question whether a proposition
has sense (Sinn) can never depend on the *truth* of another proposition about
a constituent of the first," cf. Wittgenstein's 7th and 8th entries on 18 June
1915, *Notebooks 1914-16,* p. 64.

It is, therefore, not surprising that the Rationalist Approach immediately became more prominent in his writings after having remained recessive in *The Philosophy of Logical Atomism*. In the lectures the spirit of Wittgenstein's argument does sometimes almost succeed in speaking through Russell's sentences, but the message is always transformed, because the point becomes epistemic rather than semantic.

There is a good example at the beginning of *Lecture III:* "There is, as you know a logical theory . . . according to which, if you really understood any one thing, you would understand everything. I think that rests upon a certain confusion of ideas. When you have acquaintance with a particular, you understand the particular itself quite fully, independently of the fact that there are a great many propositions about it that you do not know, but propositions about the particular are not necessary to be known in order that you should know what the particular itself is. It is rather the other way round. In order to understand a proposition in which a name of a particular occurs, you must already be acquainted with that particular. The acquaintance with the simpler is presupposed in the understanding of the more complex. . . ."[56]

Apparently, his reaction to Wittgenstein's argument when he read it in the *Tractatus* was agreement. For he summarizes it and does not express dissent from it: "The assertion that there is a certain complex reduces to the assertion that its constituents are related in a certain way, which is the assertion of a *fact;* thus if we give a name to the complex, the name only has meaning in virtue of the truth of a certain proposition, namely the proposition asserting the relatedness of the constituents of the complex. Thus the naming of complexes presupposes propositions while propositions presuppose the naming of simples."[57]

---

[56]*The Philosophy of Logical Atomism,* pp. 65-66.

[57]Russell's *Introduction* to Wittgenstein, *Tractatus Logico-Philosophicus,* London. First English Edition, 1922, p.xiii.

This was the turning-point after which the Rationalist Approach began to dominate Russell's writings on this topic. Two years later, in *Logical Atomism,* he hints at the possibility that there might be two degrees of atomicity, one absolute and the other relative to us.[58]

Sixty years later, when we look back on the development of Russell's logical atomism, the most interesting feature of the theory is this gap which seemed to him to be opening up between the phenomenal analysis of a word and its deep analysis. A doubt has already been raised about his preference for phenomenal analyses. Is the ability to recognize a shade of colour quite so large a part of knowing the meaning of the colour-word? If we ask the same question about words designating natural kinds, it might well get the negative answer that Kripke and Putnam give it.[59] The meanings of such words seem to be tied to the essences of the things even before we have discovered them, and the phenomenal properties by which we recognize them seem to belong to them only contingently and peripherally.

Today we can see the germ of this idea in Wittgenstein's *Tractatus.* Russell treated determinate shades of colour as logical atoms, because, although they are logically connected with one another, the connections cannot be used by anyone trying to learn the meaning of a colour-word on the basis of acquaintance with a different colour. Wittgenstein rejected this identification of logical atoms and insisted on a more stringent criterion of simplicity: the name of one simple thing must not be logically connected in any way with the name of any other simple thing—not even in a way which could not be used to learn the meaning of the word without acquaintance with the thing designated by it.

---

[58]Below, p. 173. Quoted above, p. 7.

[59]S. Kripke: *Naming and Necessity,* pp. 116-139; H. Putnam: *Dreaming and 'Depth Grammar'* in *Philosophical Papers Vol. II,* pp. 310-315, and *The Meaning of 'Meaning,' ibid.,* pp. 229-257.

So Wittgenstein detached logical analysis from the way in which we learn meanings in daily life. Like Putnam, he thought that the meaning of a word might be tied to the essence of the thing designated by it even though the essence had not yet been discovered. The difference is that Putnam uses scientific theory as a guide to essence, whereas Wittgenstein simply relied on the picture of logical analysis as a special kind of taking to pieces, but found in the end that it gave him no guidance. Russell has the same picture of logical analysis, but his use of it was controlled by his empiricism and so it did not lead him so far afield.

Christ Church, Oxford                                  David Pears
August, 1985

# 1918

# The Philosophy
# of Logical Atomism

The following [is the text] of a course of eight lectures delivered in [Gordon Square] London, in the first months of 1918, [which] are very largely concerned with explaining certain ideas which I learnt from my friend and former pupil Ludwig Wittgenstein. I have had no opportunity of knowing his views since August 1914, and I do not even know whether he is alive or dead. He has therefore no responsibility for what is said in these lectures beyond that of having originally supplied many of the theories contained in them.[1]

## I. Facts and Propositions

This course of lectures which I am now beginning I have called the Philosophy of Logical Atomism. Perhaps I had better begin by saying a word or two as to what I understand by that title. The kind of philosophy that I wish to advocate, which I call Logical Atomism, is one which has forced itself upon me in the course of thinking about the philosophy of mathematics, although I should find it hard to say exactly how far there is a definite logical connection between the two. The things I am going to say in these lectures are mainly my own personal opinions and I do not claim that they are more than that.

---

[1]Written as a preface to publication in *The Monist.*

As I have attempted to prove in *The Principles of Mathematics,* when we analyse mathematics we bring it all back to logic. It all comes back to logic in the strictest and most formal sense. In the present lectures, I shall try to set forth in a sort of outline, rather briefly and rather unsatisfactorily, a kind of logical doctrine which seems to me to result from the philosophy of mathematics—not exactly logically, but as what emerges as one reflects: a certain kind of logical doctrine, and on the basis of this a certain kind of metaphysic. The logic which I shall advocate is atomistic, as opposed to the monistic logic of the people who more or less follow Hegel. When I say that my logic is atomistic, I mean that I share the common-sense belief that there are many separate things; I do not regard the apparent multiplicity of the world as consisting merely in phases and unreal divisions of a single indivisible Reality. It results from that, that a considerable part of what one would have to do to justify the sort of philosophy I wish to advocate would consist in justifying the process of analysis. One is often told that the process of analysis is falsification, that when you analyse any given concrete whole you falsify it and that the results of analysis are not true. I do not think that is a right view. I do not mean to say, of course, and nobody would maintain, that when you have analysed you keep everything that you had before you analysed. If you did, you would never attain anything in analysing. I do not propose to meet the views that I disagree with by controversy, by arguing against those views, but rather by positively setting forth what I believe to be the truth about the matter, and endeavouring all the way through to make the views that I advocate result inevitably from absolutely undeniable data. When I talk of 'undeniable data' that is not to be regarded as synonymous with 'true data', because 'undeniable' is a psychological term and 'true' is not. When I say that something is 'undeniable', I mean that it is not the sort of thing that anybody is going to deny; it does not follow from that that it is true, though it does follow that we shall all think it true—and that is as near to truth as we seem able to get. When you are considering any sort of theory of knowledge, you are more or less tied to a certain unavoidable subjectivity, because you are not concerned simply with the question what is true of the world, but 'What can I know of the world?' You always have to start any kind of argument from something which appears to you to be true; if it appears to you to be true, there is no more to be done. You cannot go outside yourself and consider abstractly whether the things that appear to you to be true are true; you may do this in a particular case, where one of your beliefs is changed in consequence of others among your beliefs.

The reason that I call my doctrine *logical* atomism is because the atoms that I wish to arrive at as the sort of last residue in analysis are logical atoms and not physical atoms. Some of them will be what I call 'particulars'—such things as little patches of colour or sounds, momentary things— and some of them will be predicates or relations and so on. The point is that the atom I wish to arrive at is the atom of logical analysis, not the atom of physical analysis.

It is a rather curious fact in philosophy that the data which are undeniable to start with are always rather vague and ambiguous. You can, for instance, say: 'There are a number of people in this room at this moment.' That is obviously in some sense undeniable. But when you come to try and define what this room is, and what it is for a person to be in a room, and how you are going to distin-guish one person from another, and so forth, you find that what you have said is most fearfully vague and that you really do not know what you meant. That is a rather singular fact, that everything you are really sure of, right off is something that you do not know the meaning of, and the moment you get a precise statement you will not be sure whether it is true or false, at least right off. The process of sound philosophizing, to my mind, consists mainly in passing from those obvious, vague, ambiguous things, that we feel quite sure of, to something precise, clear, definite, which by reflection and analysis we find is involved in the vague thing that we start from, and is, so to speak, the real truth of which that vague thing is a sort of shadow. I should like, if time were longer and if I knew more than I do, to spend a whole lecture on the conception of vagueness. I think vagueness is very much more important in the theory of knowledge than you would judge it to be from the writings of most people. Everything is vague to a degree you do not realize till you have tried to make it precise, and everything precise is so remote from everything that we normally think, that you cannot for a moment suppose that is what we really mean when we say what we think.

When you pass from the vague to the precise by the method of analysis and reflection that I am speaking of, you always run a certain risk of error. If I start with the statement that there are so and so many people in this room, and then set to work to make that statement precise, I shall run a great many risks and it will be extremely likely that any precise statement I make will be something not true at all. So you cannot very easily or simply get from these vague undeniable things to precise things which are going to retain the undeniability of the starting-point. The precise propositions that you arrive at may be *logically* premisses to the system that you build up upon the basis of them, but they are not premisses for the theory of knowledge. It is important to realize the difference between that from which your knowledge is, in fact, derived, and that from which, if you already had complete knowledge, you would deduce it. Those are quite different things. The sort of premiss that a logician will take for a science will not be the sort of thing which is first known or easiest known: it will be a proposition having great deductive power, great cogency, and exactitude, quite a different thing from the actual premiss that your knowledge started from. When you are talking of the premiss for theory of knowledge, you are not talking of anything objective, but of something that will vary from man to man, because the premisses of one man's theory of knowledge will not be

the same as those of another man's. There is a great tend-
ency among a very large school to suppose that when you
are trying to philosophize about what you know, you ought
to carry back your premises further and further into the
region of the inexact and vague, beyond the point where
you yourself are, right back to the child or monkey, and
that anything whatsoever that *you* seem to know—but that
the psychologist recognizes as being the product of previous thought and analysis and reflection on your part—
cannot really be taken as a premiss in your own knowledge. That, I say, is a theory which is very widely held and
which is used against that kind of analytic outlook which
I wish to urge. It seems to me that when your object is, not
simply to study the history or development of mind, but
to ascertain the nature of the world, you do not want to
go any further back than you are already yourself. You do
not want to go back to the vagueness of the child or
monkey, because you will find that quite sufficient difficulty
is raised by your own vagueness. But there one is confronted by one of those difficulties that occur constantly in
philosophy, where you have two ultimate prejudices conflict-
ing and where argument ceases. There is the type of mind
which considers that what is called primitive experience
must be a better guide to wisdom than the experience of
reflective persons, and there is the type of mind which
takes exactly the opposite view. On that point I cannot see
any argument whatsoever. It is quite clear that a highly
educated person sees, hears, feels, does everything in a
very different way from a young child or animal, and that
this whole manner of experiencing the world and of thinking about the world is very much more analytic than that
of a more primitive experience. The things we have got to
take as premisses in any kind of work of analysis are the
things which appear to *us* undeniable—to us here and
now, as we are—and I think on the whole that the sort of
method adopted by Descartes is right: that you should set
to work to doubt things and retain only what you cannot
doubt because of its clearness and distinctness, not because

you are sure not to be induced into error, for there does not exist a method which will safeguard you against the possibility of error. The wish for perfect security is one of those snares we are always falling into, and is just as untenable in the realm of knowledge as in everything else. Nevertheless, granting all this, I think that Descartes's method is on the whole a sound one for the starting-point.

I propose, therefore, always to begin any argument that I have to make by appealing to data which will be quite ludicrously obvious. Any philosophical skill that is required will consist in the selection of those which are capable of yielding a good deal of reflection and analysis, and in the reflection and analysis themselves.

What I have said so far is by way of introduction.

The first truism to which I wish to draw your attention—and I hope you will agree with me that these things that I call truisms are so obvious that it is almost laughable to mention them—is that the world contains *facts,* which are what they are whatever we may choose to think about them, and that there are also *beliefs,* which have reference to facts, and by reference to facts are either true or false. I will try first of all to give you a preliminary explanation of what I mean by a 'fact'. When I speak of a fact—I do not propose to attempt an exact definition, but an explanation, so that you will know what I am talking about—I mean the kind of thing that makes a proposition true or false. If I say 'It is raining', what I say is true in a certain condition of weather and is false in other conditions of weather. The condition of weather that makes my statement true (or false as the case may be), is what I should call a 'fact'. If I say, 'Socrates is dead', my statement will be true owing to a certain physiological occurrence which happened in Athens long ago. If I say, 'Gravitation varies inversely as the square of the distance', my statement is rendered true by astronomical fact. If I say, 'Two and two are four', it is arithmetical fact that makes my statement true. On the other hand, if I say, 'Socrates is alive', or 'Gravitation varies directly as the distance', or 'Two and two are five', the very same facts which made my previous statements true show that these new statements are false.

I want you to realize that when I speak of a fact I do not mean a particular existing thing, such as Socrates or the rain or the sun. Socrates himself does not render any statement true or false. You might be inclined to suppose that all by himself he would give truth to the statement 'Socrates existed', but as a matter of fact that is a mistake. It is due to a confusion which I shall try to explain in the sixth lecture of this course, when I come to deal with the notion of existence. Socrates[2] himself, or any particular thing just by itself, does not make any proposition true or false. 'Socrates is dead' and 'Socrates is alive' are both of them statements about Socrates. One is true and the other false. What I call a fact is the sort of thing that is expressed by a whole sentence, not by a single name like 'Socrates'. When a single word does come to express a fact, like 'fire' or 'wolf', it is always due to an unexpressed context, and the full expression of a fact will always involve a sentence. We express a fact, for example, when we say that a certain thing has a certain property, or that it has a certain relation to another thing; but the thing which has the property or the relation is not what I call a 'fact'.

It is important to observe that facts belong to the objective world. They are not created by our thought or beliefs except in special cases. That is one of the sort of things which I should set up as an obvious truism, but, of course, one is aware, the moment one has read any philosophy at all, how very much there is to be said before such a statement as that can become the kind of position that you want. The first thing I want to emphasize is that the outer world—the world, so to speak, which knowledge is aiming at knowing—is not completely described by a lot of 'particulars', but that you must also take account of these things

---

[2]I am here for the moment treating Socrates as a 'particular'. But we shall see shortly that this view requires modification.

that I call facts, which are the sort of things that you express by a sentence, and that these, just as much as particular chairs and tables, are part of the real world. Except in psychology, most of our statements are not intended merely to express our condition of mind, though that is often all that they succeed in doing. They are intended to express facts, which (except when they are psychological facts) will be about the outer world. There are such facts involved, equally when we speak truly and when we speak falsely. When we speak falsely it is an objective fact that makes what we say false, and it is an objective fact which makes what we say true when we speak truly.

There are a great many different kinds of facts, and we shall be concerned in later lectures with a certain amount of classification of facts. I will just point out a few kinds of facts to begin with, so that you may not imagine that facts are all very much alike. There are *particular facts,* such as 'This is white'; then there are *general facts,* such as 'All men are mortal'. Of course, the distinction between particular and general facts is one of the most important. There again it would be a very great mistake to suppose that you could describe the world completely by means of particular facts alone. Suppose that you had succeeded in chronicling every single particular fact throughout the universe, and that there did not exist a single particular fact of any sort anywhere that you had not chronicled, you still would not have got a complete description of the universe unless you also added: 'These that I have chronicled are all the particular facts there are.' So you cannot hope to describe the world completely without having general facts as well as particular facts. Another distinction, which is perhaps a little more difficult to make, is between positive facts and negative facts, such as 'Socrates was alive'—a positive fact— and 'Socrates is not alive'—you might say a negative fact.[3] But the distinction is difficult to make precise. Then there

---

[3]Negative facts are further discussed in a later lecture.

are facts concerning particular things or particular qualities or relations, and, apart from them, the completely general facts of the sort that you have in logic, where there is no mention of any constituent whatever of the actual world, no mention of any particular thing or particular quality or particular relation, indeed strictly you may say no mention of anything. That is one of the characteristics of logical propositions, that they mention nothing. Such a proposition is: 'If one class is part of another, a term which is a member of the one is also a member of the other.' All those words that come in the statement of a pure logical proposition are words really belonging to syntax. They are words merely expressing form or connection, not mentioning any particular constituent of the proposition in which they occur. This is, of course, a thing that wants to be proved; I am not laying it down as self-evident. Then there are facts about the properties of single things; and facts about the relations between two things, three things, and so on; and any number of different classifications of some of the facts in the world, which are important for different purposes.

It is obvious that there is not a dualism of true and false facts; there are only just facts. It would be a mistake, of course, to say that all facts are true. That would be a mistake because true and false are correlatives, and you would only say of a thing that it was true if it was the sort of thing that *might* be false. A fact cannot be either true or false. That brings us on to the question of statements or propositions or judgments, all those things that do have the quality of truth and falsehood. For the purposes of logic, though not, I think, for the purposes of theory of knowledge, it is natural to concentrate upon the proposition as the thing which is going to be our typical vehicle on the duality of truth and falsehood. A proposition, one may say, is a sentence in the indicative, a sentence asserting something, not questioning or commanding or wishing. It may also be a sentence of that sort preceded by the word 'that'. For example, 'That Socrates is alive', 'That two and two are four', 'That two and two are five', anything of that sort will be a proposition.

A proposition is just a symbol. It is a complex symbol in the sense that it has parts which are also symbols: a symbol may be defined as complex when it has parts that are symbols. In a sentence containing several words, the several words are each symbols, and the sentence comprising them is therefore a complex symbol in that sense. There is a good deal of importance to philosophy in the theory of symbolism, a good deal more than one time I thought. I think the importance is almost entirely negative, i.e., the importance lies in the fact that unless you are fairly self-conscious about symbols, unless you are fairly aware of the relation of the symbol to what it symbolizes, you will find yourself attributing to the thing properties which only belong to the symbol. That, of course, is especially likely in very abstract studies such as philosophical logic, because the subject-matter that you are supposed to be thinking of is so exceedingly difficult and elusive that any person who has ever tried to think about it knows you do not think about it except perhaps once in six months for half a minute. The rest of the time you think about the symbols, because they are tangible, but the thing you are supposed to be thinking about is fearfully difficult and one does not often manage to think about it. The really good philosopher is the one who does once in six months think about it for a minute. Bad philosophers never do. That is why the theory of symbolism has a certain importance, because otherwise you are so certain to mistake the properties of the symbolism for the properties of the thing. It has other interesting sides to it too. There are different kinds of symbols, different kinds of relation between symbol and what is symbolized, and very important fallacies arise from not realizing this. The sort of contradictions about which I shall be speaking in connection with types in a later lecture all arise from mistakes in symbolism, from putting one sort of symbol in the place where another sort of symbol ought to be. Some of the notions that have been thought absolutely fundamental in philosophy have arisen, I believe, entirely through mistakes as to symbolism—e.g. the notion of existence, or, if you like, reality. Those two words stand for a great deal that has been discussed in philosophy. There has been the theory about every proposition being really a description of reality as a whole and so on, and altogether these notions of reality and existence have played a very prominent part in philosophy. Now my own belief is that as they have occurred in philosophy, they have been entirely the outcome of a muddle about symbolism, and that when you have cleared up that muddle, you find that practically everythng that has been said about existence is sheer and simple mistake, and that is all you can say about it. I shall go into that in a later lecture, but it is an example of the way in which symbolism is important.

Perhaps I ought to say a word or two about what I am understanding by symbolism, because I think some people think you only mean mathematical symbols when you talk about symbolism. I am using it in a sense to include all language of every sort and kind, so that every word is a symbol, and every sentence, and so forth. When I speak of a symbol I simply mean something that 'means' something else, and as to what I mean by 'meaning' I am not prepared to tell you. I will in the course of time enumerate a strictly infinite number of different things that 'meaning' may mean but I shall not consider that I have exhausted the discussion by doing that. I think that the notion of meaning is always more or less psychological, and that it is not possible to get a pure logical theory of meaning, nor therefore of symbolism. I think that it is of the very essence of the explanation of what you mean by a symbol to take account of such things as knowing, of cognitive relations, and probably also of association. At any rate I am pretty clear that the theory of symbolism and the use of symbolism is not a thing that can be explained in pure logic without taking account of the various cognitive relations that you may have to things.

As to what one means by 'meaning', I will give a few illustrations. For instance, the word 'Socrates', you will say, means a certain man; the word 'mortal' means a certain quality; and the sentence 'Socrates is mortal' means a certain fact. But these three sorts of meaning are entirely distinct, and you will get into the most hopeless contradictions if you think the word 'meaning' has the same meaning in each of these three cases. It is very important not to suppose that there is just one thing which is meant by 'meaning', and that therefore there is just one sort of relation of the symbol to what is symbolized. A name would be a proper symbol to use for a person; a sentence (or a proposition) is the proper symbol for a fact.

A belief or a statement has duality of truth and falsehood, which the fact does not have. A belief or a statement always involves a proposition. You say that a man believes that so and so is the case. A man believes that Socrates is dead. What he believes is a proposition on the face of it, and for formal purposes it is convenient to take the proposition as the essential thing having the duality of truth and falsehood. It is very important to realize such things, for instance, as that *propositions are not names for facts*. It is quite obvious as soon as it is pointed out to you, but as a matter of fact I never had realized it until it was pointed out to me by a former pupil of mine, Wittgenstein. It is perfectly evident as soon as you think of it, that a proposition is not a name for a fact, from the mere circumstance that there are *two* propositions corresponding to each fact. Suppose it is a fact that Socrates is dead. You have two propositions: 'Socrates is dead' and 'Socrates is not dead'. And those two propositions corresponding to the same fact; there is one fact in the world which makes one true and one false. That is not accidental, and illustrates how the relation of proposition to fact is a totally different one from the relation of name to the thing named. For each fact there are two propositions, one true and one false, and there is nothing in the nature of the symbol to show us which is the true one and which is the false one. If there were, you could

ascertain the truth about the world by examining propositions without looking around you.

There are two different relations, as you see, that a
proposition may have to a fact: the one the relation that
you may call being true to the fact, and the other being
false to the fact. Both are equally essentially logical relations which may subsist between the two, whereas in the
case of a name, there is only one relation that it can have
to what it names. A name can just name a particular, or,
if it does not, it is not a name at all, it is a noise. It cannot
be a name without having just that one particular relation
of naming a certain thing, whereas a proposition does not
cease to be a proposition if it is false. It has two ways, of
being true and being false, which together correspond to
the property of being a name. Just as a word may be a
name or be not a name but just a meaningless noise, so
a phrase which is apparently a proposition may be either
true or false, or may be meaningless, but the true and false
belong together as against the meaningless. That shows,
of course, that the formal logical characteristics of propositions are quite different from those of names, and that the
relations they have to facts are quite different, and therefore propositions are not names for facts. You must not
run away with the idea that you can name facts in any
other way; you cannot. You cannot name them at all. You
cannot properly name a fact. The only thing you can do
is to assert it, or deny it, or desire it, or will it, or wish it,
or question it, but all those are things involving the whole
proposition. You can never put the sort of thing that makes
a proposition to be true or false in the position of a logical
subject. You can only have it there as something to be
asserted or denied or something of that sort, but not something to be named.

*Discussion*

*Question:* Do you take your starting-point 'That there
are many things' as a postulate which is to be carried along
all through, or has to be proved afterwards?

*Mr. Russell:* No, neither the one nor the other. I do not take it as a postulate that 'There are many things'. I should take it that, in so far as it can be proved, the proof is empirical, and that the disproofs that have been offered are *a priori*. The empirical person would naturally say, there are many things. The monistic philosopher attempts to show that there are not. I should propose to refute his *a priori* arguments. I do not consider there is any *logical* necessity for there to be many things, nor for there not to be many things.

*Question:* I mean in making a start, whether you start with the empirical or the *a priori* philosophy, do you make your statement just at the beginning and come back to prove it, or do you never come back to the proof of it?

*Mr. Russell:* No, you never come back. It is like the acorn to the oak. You never get back to the acorn in the oak. I should like a statement which would be rough and vague and have that sort of obviousness that belongs to things of which you never know what they mean, but I should never get back to that statement. I should say, here is a thing. We seem somehow convinced that there is truth buried in this thing somewhere. We will look at it inside and out until we have extracted something and can say, now that is true. It will not really be the same as the thing we started from because it will be so much more analytic and precise.

*Question:* Does it not look as though you could name a fact by a date?

*Mr. Russell:* You can apparently name facts, but I do not think you can really: you always find that if you set out the whole thing fully, it was not so. Suppose you say 'The death of Socrates'. You might say, that is a name for the fact that Socrates died. But it obviously is not. You can see that the moment you take account of truth and falsehood. Supposing he had not died, the phrase would still be just as significant although there could not be then anything you could name. But supposing he had never lived, the sound 'Socrates' would not be a name at all. You can see it in another way. You can say 'The death of Socrates is a fiction'. Suppose you had read in the paper that the Kaiser had been assassinated, and it turned out to be not true. You could then say, 'The death of the Kaiser is a fiction'. It is clear that there is no such thing in the world as a fiction, and yet that statement is a perfectly sound statement. From this it follows that 'The death of the Kaiser' is not a name.

## II. Particulars, Predicates, and Relations

I propose to begin today the analysis of facts and propositions, for in a way the chief thesis that I have to maintain is the legitimacy of analysis, because if one goes into what I call Logical Atomism that means that one does believe the world can be analysed into a number of separate things with relations and so forth, and that the sort of arguments that many philosophers use against analysis are not justifiable.

In a philosophy of logical atomism one might suppose that the first thing to do would be to discover the kinds of atoms out of which logical structures are composed. But I do not think that is quite the first thing; it is one of the early things, but not quite the first. There are two other questions that one has to consider, and one of these at least is prior. You have to consider:

1. Are the things that look like logically complex entities really complex?
2. Are they really entities?

The second question we can put off; in fact, I shall not deal with it fully until my last lecture. The first question, whether they are really complex, is one that you have to consider at the start. Neither of these questions is, as it stands, a very precise question. I do not pretend to start with precise questions. I do not think you can start with anything precise. You have to achieve such precision as you can, as you go along. Each of these two questions, however, is *capable* of a precise meaning, and each is really important.

There is another question which comes still earlier, namely: what shall we take as prima facie examples of logically complex entities? That really is the first question of all to start with. What sort of things shall we regard as prima facie complex?

Of course, all the ordinary objects of daily life are apparently complex entities: such things as tables and chairs, loaves and fishes, persons and principalities and powers— they are all on the face of it complex entities. All the kinds of things to which we habitually give proper names are on the face of them complex entities: Socrates, Piccadilly, Rumania, Twelfth Night or anything you like to think of, to which you give a proper name, they are all apparently complex entities. They seem to be complex systems bound together into some kind of a unity, that sort of a unity that leads to the bestowal of a single appellation. I think it is the contemplation of this sort of apparent unity which has very largely led to the philosophy of monism, and to the suggestion that the universe as a whole is a single complex entity more or less in the sense in which these things are that I have been talking about.

For my part, I do not believe in complex entities of this kind, and it is not such things as these that I am going to take as the prima facie examples of complex entities. My reasons will appear more and more plainly as I go on. I cannot give them all today, but I can more or less explain what I mean in a preliminary way. Suppose, for example, that you were to analyse what appears to be a fact about Piccadilly. Suppose you made any statement about Piccadilly, such as: 'Piccadilly is a pleasant street.' If you analyse a statement of that sort correctly, I believe you will find that the fact corresponding to your statement does not contain any constituent corresponding to the word 'Piccadilly'. The word 'Piccadilly' will form part of many significant propositions, but the facts corresponding to these propositions do not contain any single constituent, whether simple or complex, corresponding to the word 'Piccadilly'. That is to say, if you take language as a guide in your analysis of the fact expressed, you will be led astray in a statement of that sort. The reasons for that I shall give at length in Lecture VI, and partly also in Lecture VII, but I could say in a preliminary way certain things that would make you understand what I mean. 'Piccadilly', on the face of it, is the name for a certain portion of the earth's surface, and I suppose, if you wanted to define it, you would have to define it as a series of classes of material entities, namely those which, at varying times, occupy that portion of the earth's surface. So that you would find that the logical status of Piccadilly is bound up with the logical status of series and classes, and if you are going to hold Piccadilly as real, you must hold that series of classes are real, and whatever sort of metaphysical status you assign to them, you must assign to it. As you know, I believe that series and classes are of the nature of logical fictions: therefore that thesis, if it can be maintained, will dissolve Piccadilly into a fiction. Exactly similar remarks will apply to other instances: Rumania, Twelfth Night, and Socrates. Socrates, perhaps, raises some special questions, because the question what constitutes a person has special difficulties in it. But, for the sake of argument, one might identify Socrates with the series of his experiences. He would be really a series of classes, because one has many experiences simultaneously. Therefore he comes to be very like Piccadilly.

Considerations of that sort seem to take us away from such prima facie complex entities as we started with to others as being more stubborn and more deserving of analytical attention, namely facts. I explained last time what I meant by a fact, namely, that sort of thing that makes a proposition true or false, the sort of thing which is the case when your statement is true and is not the case when your statement is false. Facts are, as I said last time, plainly something you have to take account of if you are going to give a complete account of the world. You cannot do that by merely enumerating the particular things that are in it: you must also mention the relations of these things, and their properties, and so forth, all of which are facts, so that facts certainly belong to an account of the objective world, and facts do seem much more clearly complex and much more not capable of being explained away than things like Socrates and Rumania. However you may explain away the meaning of the word 'Socrates', you will still be left with the truth that the proposition 'Socrates is mortal' expresses a fact. You may not know exactly what Socrates means, but it is quite clear that 'Socrates is mortal' does express a fact. There is clearly some valid meaning in saying that the fact expressed by 'Socrates is mortal' is *complex*. The things in the world have various properties, and stand in various relations to each other. That they have these properties and relations are *facts,* and the things and their qualities or relations are quite clearly in some sense or other components of the facts that have those qualities or relations. The analysis of apparently complex *things* such as we started with can be reduced by various means, to the analysis of facts which are apparently about those things. Therefore it is with the analysis of *facts* that one's consideration of the problem of complexity must begin, not with the analysis of apparently complex things.

The complexity of a fact is evidenced, to begin with, by the circumstance that the proposition which asserts a fact consists of several words, each of which may occur in other contexts. Of course, sometimes you get a proposition expressed by a single word but if it is expressed fully it is bound to contain several words. The proposition 'Socrates is mortal' may be replaced by 'Plato is mortal' or by 'Socrates is human'; in the first case we alter the subject, in the second the predicate. It is clear that all the propositions in which the word 'Socrates' occurs have something in common, and again all the propositions in which the word 'mortal' occurs have something in common, something which they do not have in common with all propositions, but only with those which are about Socrates or mortality. It is clear, I think, that the facts corresponding to propositions in which the word 'Socrates' occurs have something in common corresponding to the common word 'Socrates' which occurs in the propositions, so that you have that sense of complexity to begin with, that in a fact you can get something which it may have in common with other facts, just as you may have 'Socrates is human' and 'Socrates is mortal', both of them facts, and both having to do with Socrates, although Socrates does not constitute the whole of either of these facts. It is quite clear that in that sense there is a possibility of cutting up a fact into component parts, of which one component may be altered without altering the others, and one component may occur in certain other facts though not in all other facts. I want to make it clear, to begin with, that there is a sense in which facts can be analysed. I am not concerned with all the difficulties of any analysis, but only with meeting the prima facie objections of philosophers who think you really cannot analyse at all.

I am trying as far as possible again this time, as I did last time, to start with perfectly plain truisms. My desire and wish is that the things I start with should be so obvious that you wonder why I spend my time stating them. This is what I aim at, because the point of philosophy is to start with something so simple as not to seem worth stating, and to end with something so paradoxical that no one will believe it.

One prima facie mark of complexity in propositions is the fact that they are expressed by several words. I come now to another point, which applies primarily to propositions and thence derivatively to facts. You can understand a proposition when you understand the words of which it is composed even though you never heard the proposition before. That seems a very humble property, but it is a property which marks it as complex and distinguishes it from words whose meaning is simple. When you know the vocabulary, grammar, and syntax of language, you can understand a proposition in that language even though you never saw it before. In reading a newspaper, for example, you become aware of a number of statements which are new to you, and they are intelligible to you immediately, in spite of the fact that they are new, because you understand the words of which they are composed. This characteristic, that you can understand a proposition through the understanding of its component words, is absent from the component words when those words express some-thing simple. Take the word 'red', for example, and sup-pose—as one always has to do—that 'red' stands for a particular shade of colour. You will pardon that assump-tion, but one never can get on otherwise. You cannot understand the meaning of the word 'red' except through seeing red things. There is no other way in which it can be done. It is no use to learn languages, or to look up diction-aries. None of these things will help you to understand the meaning of the word 'red'. In that way it is quite different from the meaning of a proposition. Of course, you can give a definition of the word 'red', and here it is very important to distinguish between a definition and an analysis. All analysis is only possible in regard to what is complex, and it always depends, in the last analysis, upon direct ac-quaintance with the objects which are the meanings of certain simple symbols. It is hardly necessary to observe that one does not define a thing but a symbol. (A 'simple' symbol is a symbol whose parts are not symbols.) A simple symbol is quite a different thing from a simple thing. Those objects which it is impossible to symbolize otherwise than by simple symbols may be called 'simple', while those which can be symbolized by a combination of symbols may be called 'complex'. This is, of course, a preliminary definition, and perhaps somewhat circular, but that doesn't much matter at this stage.

I have said that 'red' could not be understood except by seeing red things. You might object to that on the ground that you can define red for example, as 'The colour with the greatest wave-length'. That, you might say, is a definition of 'red' and a person could understand that definition even if he had seen nothing red, provided he understood the physical theory of colour. But that does not really constitute the meaning of the word 'red' in the very *diff fact ?*

slightest. If you take such a proposition as 'This is red' and substitute for it 'This has the colour with the greatest wave-length', you have a different proposition altogether. You can see that at once, because a person who knows nothing of the physical theory of colour can undertand the proposition 'This is red', and can know that it is true, but cannot know that 'This has the colour which has the greatest wave-length'. Conversely, you might have a hypothetical person who could not see red, but who understood the physical theory of colour and could apprehend the proposition 'This has the colour with the greatest wave-length', but who would not be able to understand the proposition 'This is red' as understood by the normal uneducated person. Therefore it is clear that if you define 'red' as 'The colour with the greatest wave-length', you are not giving the actual meaning of the word at all; you are simply giving a true description, which is quite a different thing, and the propositions which result are different propositions from those in which the word 'red' occurs. In that sense the word 'red' cannot be defined, though in the sense in which a correct description constitutes a definition it can be defined. In the sense of analysis you cannot define 'red'. That is how it is that dictionaries are able to get on, because a dictionary professes to define all words in the language by means of words in the language, and therefore it is clear that a dictionary must be guilty of a vicious circle somewhere, but it manages it by means of correct descriptions.

*test*

I have made it clear, then, in what sense I should say that the word 'red' is a simple symbol and the phrase 'This is red' a complex symbol. The word 'red' can only be understood through acquaintance with the object, whereas the phrase 'Roses are red' can be understood if you know what 'red' is and what 'roses' are, without ever having heard the phrase before. That is a clear mark of what is complex. It is the mark of a complex symbol, and also the mark of the object symbolized by the complex symbol. That is to say, propositions are complex symbols, and the facts they stand for are complex.

The whole question of the meaning of words is very full of complexities and ambiguities in ordinary language. When one person uses a word, he does not mean by it the same thing as another person means by it. I have often heard it said that that is a misfortune. That is a mistake. It would be absolutely fatal if people meant the same things by their words. It would make all intercourse impossible, and language the most hopeless and useless thing imaginable, because the meaning you attach to your words must depend on the nature of the objects you are acquainted with, and since different people are acquainted with different objects, they would not be able to talk to each other unless they attached quite different meanings to their words. We should have to talk only about logic—a not wholly undesirable result. Take, for example, the word 'Piccadilly'. We, who are acquainted with Piccadilly, attach quite a different meaning to that word from any which could be attached to it by a person who had never been in London: and, supposing that you travel in foreign parts and expatiate on Piccadilly, you will convey to your hearers entirely different propositions from those in your mind. They will know Piccadilly as an important street in London; they may know a lot about it, but they will not know just the things one knows when one is walking along it. If you were to insist on language which was unambiguous, you would be unable to tell people at home what you had seen in foreign parts. It would be altogether incredibly inconvenient to have an unambiguous language, and therefore mercifully we have not got one.

Analysis is not the same thing as definition. You can define a term by means of a correct description, but that does not constitute an analysis. It is analysis, not definition, that we are concerned with at the present moment, so I will come back to the question of analysis.

We may lay down the following provisional definitions:

That the components of a proposition are the symbols we must understand in
    order to understand the proposition;
That the components of the fact which makes a proposition true or false, as the
    case may be, are the *meanings* of the symbols which we must understand
    in order to understand the proposition.

That is not absolutely correct, but it will enable you to
understand my meaning. One reason why it fails of cor-
rectness is that it does not apply to words which, like 'or'
and 'not', are parts of propositions without corresponding
to any part of the corresponding facts. This is a topic for
Lecture III.

I call these definitions *preliminary* because they start
from the complexity of the proposition, which they define
psychologically, and proceed to the complexity of the fact,
whereas it is quite clear that in an orderly, proper procedure it is the complexity of the fact that you would start
from. It is also clear that the complexity of the fact cannot
be something merely psychological. If in astronomical fact
the earth moves round the sun, that is genuinely complex.
It is not that you think it complex, it is a sort of genuine
objective complexity, and therefore one ought in a proper,
orderly procedure to start from the complexity of the
world and arrive at the complexity of the proposition. The
only reason for going the other way round is that in all
abstract matters symbols are easier to grasp. I doubt, however, whether complexity, in that fundamental objective
sense in which one starts from complexity of a fact, is
definable at all. You cannot analyse what you mean by
complexity in that sense. You must just apprehend it—at
least so I am inclined to think. There is nothing one could
say about it, beyond giving criteria such as I have been
giving. Therefore, when you cannot get a real proper analysis of a thing, it is generally best to talk round it without
professing that you have given an exact definition.

It might be suggested that complexity is essentially to
do with symbols, or that it is essentially psychological. I do
not think it would be possible seriously to maintain either
of these views, but they are the sort of views that will occur

to one, the sort of thing that one would try, to see whether it would work. I do not think they will do at all. When we come to the principles of symbolism which I shall deal with in Lecture VII, I shall try to persuade you that in a logically correct symbolism there will always be a certain fundamental identity of structure between a fact and the symbol for it; and that the complexity of the symbol corresponds very closely with the complexity of the facts symbolized by it. Also, as I said before, it is quite directly evident to inspection that the fact, for example, that two things stand in a certain relation to one another—e.g. that this is to the left of that—is itself objectively complex, and not merely that the apprehension of it is complex. The fact that two things stand in a certain relation to each other, or any statement of that sort, has a complexity all of its own. I shall therefore in future assume that there is an objective complexity in the world, and that it is mirrored by the complexity of propositions.

A moment ago I was speaking about the great advantages that we derive from the logical imperfections of language, from the fact that our words are all ambiguous. I propose now to consider what sort of language a logically perfect language would be. In a logically perfect language the words in a proposition would correspond one by one with the components of the corresponding fact, with the exception of such words as 'or', 'not', 'if', 'then', which have a different function. In a logically perfect language, there will be one word and no more for every simple object, and everything that is not simple will be expressed by a combination of words, by a combination derived, of course, from the words for the simple things that enter in, one word for each simple component. A language of that sort will be completely analytic, and will show at a glance the logical structure of the facts asserted or denied. The language which is set forth in *Principia Mathematica* is intended to be a language of that sort. It is a language which has only syntax and no vocabulary whatsoever. Barring the omission of a vocabulary I maintain that it is quite a nice language. It aims at being the sort of a language that, if you add a vocabulary, would be a logically perfect language. Actual languages are not logically perfect in this sense, and they cannot possibly be, if they are to serve the purposes of daily life. A logically perfect language, if it could be constructed, would not only be intolerably prolix, but, as regards its vocabulary, would be very largely private to one speaker. That is to say, all the names that it would use would be private to that speaker and could not enter into the language of another speaker. It could not use proper names for Socrates or Piccadilly or Rumania for the reasons which I went into earlier in the lecture. Altogether you would find that it would be a very inconvenient language indeed. That is one reason why logic is so very backward as a science, because the needs of logic are so extraordinarily different from the needs of daily life. One wants a language in both, and unfortunately it is logic that has to give way, not daily life. I shall, however, assume that we have constructed a logically perfect language, and that we are going on State occasions to use it, and I will now come back to the question which I intended to start with, namely, the analysis of facts.

The simplest imaginable facts are those which consist in the possession of a quality by some particular thing. Such facts, say, as 'This is white'. They have to be taken in a very sophisticated sense. I do not want you to think about the piece of chalk I am holding, but of what you see when you look at the chalk. If one says, 'This is white' it will do for about as simple a fact as you can get hold of. The next simplest would be those in which you have a relation between two facts, such as: 'This is to the left of that.' Next you come to those where you have a triadic relation between three particulars. (An instance which Royce gives as 'A gives B to C.') So you get relations which require as their minimum three terms, those we call triadic relations; and those which require four terms, which we call tetradic, and so on. There you have a whole infinite hierarchy of facts—facts in which you have a thing and a quality, two things and a relation, three things and a relation, four things and a relation, and so on. That whole hierarchy constitutes what I call _atomic_ facts, and they are the simplest sort of fact. You can distinguish among them some simpler than others, because the ones containing a quality are simpler than those in which you have, say, a pentadic relation, and so on. The whole lot of them, taken together, are as facts go very simple, and are what I call atomic facts. The propositions expressing them are what I call _atomic propositions_.

In every atomic fact there is one component which is naturally expressed by a verb (or, in the case of quality, it may be expressed by a predicate, by an adjective). This one component is a quality or dyadic or triadic or tetradic . . . relation. It would be very convenient, for purposes of talking about these matters, to call a quality a 'monadic relation' and I shall do so; it saves a great deal of circumlocution.

In that case you can say that all atomic propositions assert relations of varying orders. Atomic facts contain, besides the relation, the terms of the relation—one term if it is a monadic relation, two if it is dyadic, and so on. These 'terms' which come into atomic facts I define as 'particulars'.

Particulars=terms of relations in atomic facts.  Df.

That is the definition of particulars, and I want to emphasize it because the definition of a particular is something purely logical. The question whether this or that is a particular, is a question to be decided in terms of that logical definition. In order to understand the definition it is not necessary to know beforehand 'This is a particular' or 'That is a particular'. It remains to be investigated what particulars you can find in the world, if any. The whole question of what particulars you actually find in the real world is a purely empirical one which does not interest the logician as such. The logician as such never gives instances, because it is one of the tests of a logical proposition that you need not know anything whatsoever about the real world in order to understand it.

Passing from atomic facts to atomic propositions, the word expressing a monadic relation or quality is called a 'predicate', and the word expressing a relation of any higher order would generally be a verb, sometimes a single verb, sometimes a whole phrase. At any rate the verb gives the essential nerve, as it were, of the relation. The other words that occur in the atomic propositions, the words that are not the predicate or verb, may be called the subjects of the proposition. There will be one subject in a monadic proposition, two in a dyadic one, and so on. The subjects in a proposition will be the words expressing the terms of the relation which is expressed by the proposition.

The only kind of word that is theoretically capable of standing for a particular is a *proper name,* and the whole matter of proper names is rather curious.

Proper names=words for particulars.  Df.

I have put that down although, as far as a common language goes, it is obviously false. It is true that if you try to think how you are to talk about particulars, you will see that you cannot ever talk about a particular particular except by means of a proper name. You cannot use general words except by way of description. How are you to express in words an atomic proposition? An atomic proposition is one which does mention actual particulars, not merely describe them but actually name them, and you can only name them by means of names. You can see at once for yourself, therefore, that every other part of speech except proper names is obviously quite incapable of standing for a particular. Yet it does seem a little odd if, having made a dot on the blackboard, I call it 'John'. You would be surprised, and yet how are you to know otherwise what it is that I am speaking of. If I say, 'The dot that is on the right-hand side is white' that is a proposition. If I say 'This is white' that is quite a different proposition. 'This' will do very well while we are all here and can see it, but if I wanted to talk about it tomorrow it would be convenient to have christened it and called it 'John'. There is no other way in which you can mention it. You cannot really mention *it* itself except by means of a name.

What pass for names in language, like 'Socrates', 'Plato', and so forth, were originally intended to fulfil this function of standing for particulars, and we do accept, in ordinary daily life, as particulars all sorts of things that really are not so. The names that we commonly use, like 'Socrates', are really abbreviations for descriptions; not only that, but what they describe are not particulars but complicated systems of classes or series. A name, in the narrow logical sense of a word whose meaning is a particular, can only be applied to a particular with which the speaker is acquainted, because you cannot name anything you are not acquainted with. You remember, when Adam named the beasts, they came before him one by one, and he became acquainted with them and named them. We are not acquainted with Socrates, and therefore cannot name him. When we use the word 'Socrates', we are really using a description. Our thought may be rendered by some such phrase as, 'The Master of Plato', or 'The philosopher who drank the hemlock', or 'The person whom logicians assert to be mortal', but we certainly do not use the name as a name in the proper sense of the word.

That makes it very difficult to get any instance of a name at all in the proper strict logical sense of the word. The only words one does use as names in the logical sense are words like 'this' or 'that'. One can use 'this' as a name to stand for a particular with which one is acquainted at the moment. We say 'This is white'. If you agree that 'This is white', meaning the 'this' that you see, you are using 'this' as a proper name. But if you try to apprehend the proposition that I am expressing when I say 'This is white', you cannot do it. If you mean this piece of chalk as a physical object, then you are not using a proper name. It is only when you use 'this' quite strictly, to stand for an actual object of sense, that it is really a proper name. And in that it has a very odd property for a proper name, namely that it seldom means the same thing two moments running and does not mean the same thing to the speaker and to the hearer. It is an *ambiguous* proper name, but it is really a proper name all the same, and it is almost the only thing I can think of that is used properly and logically in the sense that I was talking of for a proper name. The importance of proper names, in the sense of which I am talking, is in the sense of logic, not of daily life. You can see why it is that in the logical language set forth in *Principia Mathematica* there are not any names, because there we are not interested in particular particulars but only in general particulars, if I may be allowed such a phrase.

Particulars have this peculiarity, among the sort of objects that you have to take account of in an inventory of the world, that each of them stands entirely alone and is completely self-subsistent. It has the sort of self-subsistence that used to belong to substance, except that it usually only persists through a very short time, so far as our experience goes. That is to say, each particular that there is in the world does not in any way logically depend upon any other particular. Each one might happen to be the whole universe; it is a merely empirical fact that this is not the case. There is no reason why you should not have a universe consisting of one particular and nothing else. That is a peculiarity of particulars. In the same way, in order to understand a name for a particular, the only thing necessary is to be acquainted with that particular. When you are acquainted with that particular, you have a full, adequate, and complete understanding of the name, and no further information is required. No further information as to the facts that are true of that particular would enable you to have a fuller understanding of the meaning of the name.

### Discussion

*Mr. Carr:* You think there are simple facts that are not complex. Are complexes all composed of simples? Are not the simples that go into complexes themselves complex?

*Mr. Russell:* <u>No facts are simple.</u> As to your second question, that is, of course, a question that might be argued—whether when a thing is complex it is necessary that it should in analysis have constituents that are simple. I think it is perfectly possible to suppose that complex things are capable of analysis *ad infinitum,* and that you never reach the simple. I do not think it is true, but it is a thing that one might argue, certainly. I do myself think that complexes—I do not like to talk of complexes— are composed of simples, but I admit that that is a difficult argument, and it might be that analysis could go on forever.

*Mr. Carr:* You do not mean that in calling the thing complex, you have asserted that there really are simples?

*Mr. Russell:* No, I do not think that is *necessarily* implied.

*Mr. Neville:* I do not feel clear that the proposition 'This is white' is in any case a simpler proposition than the proposition 'This and that have the same colour'.

*Mr. Russell:* That is one of the things I have not had time for. It may be the same as the proposition 'This and that have the same colour.' It may be that white is defined as the colour of 'this', or rather that the proposition 'This is white' means 'This is identical in colour with that', the colour of 'that' being, so to speak, the definition of white. That may be, but there is no special reason to think that it is.

*Mr. Neville:* Are there any monadic relations which would be better examples?

*Mr. Russell:* I think not. It is perfectly obvious *a priori* that you can get rid of all monadic relations by that trick. One of the things I was going to say if I had had time was that you can get rid of dyadic and reduce to triadic, and so on. But there is no particular reason to suppose that that is the way the world begins, that it begins with relations of order *n* instead of relations of order I. You cannot reduce them downward, but you can reduce them upward.

*Question:* If the proper name of a thing, a 'this', varies from instant to instant, how is it possible to make any argument?

*Mr. Russell:* You can keep 'this' going for about a minute or two. I made that dot and talked about it for some little time. I mean it varies often. If you argue quickly, you can get some little way before it is finished. I think things last for a finite time, a matter of some seconds or minutes or whatever it may happen to be.

*Question:* You do not think that air is acting on that and changing it?

*Mr. Russell:* It does not matter about that if it does not alter its appearance enough for you to have a different sense-datum.

## III. Atomic and Molecular Propositions

I did not quite finish last time the syllabus that I intended for Lecture II, so I must first do that.

I had been speaking at the end of my last lecture on the subject of the self-subsistence of particulars, how each particular has its being independently of any other and does not depend upon anything else for the logical possibility of its existence. I compared particulars with the old conception of substance, that is to say, they have the quality of self-subsistence that used to belong to substance, but not the quality of persistence through time. A particular, as a rule, is apt to last for a very short time indeed, not an instant but a very short time. In that respect particulars differ from the old substances but in their logical position they do not. There is, as you know, a logical theory which is quite opposed to that view, a logical theory according to which, if you really understood any one thing, you would understand everything. I think that rests upon a certain confusion of ideas. When you have acquaintance with a particular, you understand that particular itself quite fully, independently of the fact that there are a great many propositions about it that you do not know, but propositions concerning the particular are not necessary to be known in order that you may know what the particular itself is. It is rather the other way round. In order to understand a proposition in which the name of a particular occurs, you must already be acquainted with that particular. The acquaintance with the simpler is presupposed in the understanding of the more complex, but the logic that I should wish to combat maintains that in order thoroughly to know any one thing, you must know all its relations and all its qualities, all the propositions in fact in which that thing is mentioned; and you deduce of course from that that the world is an interdependent whole. It is on a basis of that sort that the logic of monism develops. Generally one supports this theory by talking about the 'nature' of a thing, assuming that a thing has something which you call its 'nature' which is generally elaborately confounded and distinguished from the thing, so that you can get a comfortable see-saw which enables you to deduce whichever results suit the moment. The 'nature' of the thing would come to mean all the true propositions in which the thing is mentioned. Of course it is clear that since everything has relations to everything else, you cannot know all the facts of which a thing is a constituent without having some knowledge of everything in the universe. When you realize that what one calls 'knowing a particular' merely means acquaintance with that particular and is presupposed in the understanding of any proposition in which that particular is mentioned, I think you also realize that you cannot take the view that the understanding of the name of the particular presupposes knowledge of all the propositions concerning that particular.

I should like to say about understanding, that that phrase is often used mistakenly. People speak of 'understanding the universe' and so on. But, of course, the only thing you can really understand (in the strict sense of the word) is a symbol, and to understand a symbol is to know what it stands for.

I pass on from particulars to predicates and relations and what we mean by understanding the words that we use for predicates and relations. A very great deal of what I am saying in this course of lectures consists of ideas which

I derived from my friend Wittgenstein. But I have had no opportunity of knowing how far his ideas have changed since August 1914, nor whether he is alive or dead, so I cannot make anyone but myself responsible for them.

Understanding a predicate is quite a different thing from understanding a name. By a predicate, as you know, I mean the word that is used to designate a quality such as red, white, square, round, and the understanding of a word like that involves a different kind of act of mind from that which is involved in understanding a name. To understand a name you must be acquainted with the particular of which it is a name, and you must know that it is the name of that particular. You do not, that is to say, have any suggestion of the form of a proposition, whereas in understanding a predicate you do. To understand 'red', for instance, is to understand what is meant by saying that a thing is red. You have to bring in the form of a proposition. You do not have to know, concerning any particular 'this', that 'This is red' but you have to know what is the meaning of saying that anything is red. You have to understand what one would call 'being red'. The importance of that is in connection with the theory of types, which I shall come to later on. It is in the fact that a predicate can never occur except as a predicate. When it seems to occur as a subject, the phrase wants amplifying and explaining, unless, of course, you are talking about the word itself. You must say ' "Red" is a predicate', but then you must have 'red' in inverted commas because you are talking about the word 'red'. When you understand 'red' it means that you understand propositions of the form that '$x$ is red'. So that the understanding of a predicate is something a little more complicated than the understanding of a name, just because of that. Exactly the same applies to relations, and in fact all those things that are not particulars. Take, e.g., 'before' in '$x$ is before $y$': you understand 'before' when you understand what that would mean if $x$ and $y$ were given. I do not mean you know whether it is true, but you understand the proposition. Here again the same thing applies. A relation can never occur except as a relation, never as a subject. You will always have to put in hypothetical terms, if not real ones, such as 'If I say that $x$ is before $y$, I assert a relation between $x$ and $y$'. It is in this way that you will have to expand such a statement as ' "Before" is a relation' in order to get its meaning.

The different sorts of words, in fact, have different sorts of uses and must be kept always to the right use and not to the wrong use, and it is fallacies arising from putting symbols to wrong uses that lead to the contradictions concerned with types.

There is just one more point before I leave the subjects I meant to have dealt with last time, and that is a point which came up in discussion at the conclusion of the last lecture, namely, that if you like you can get a formal reduction of (say) monadic relations to dyadic, or of dyadic to triadic, or of all the relations below a certain order to all above that order, but the converse reduction is not possible. Suppose one takes, for example, 'red'. One says, 'This is red', 'That is red', and so forth. Now, if anyone is of the opinion that there is reason to try to get on without subject-predicate propositions, all that is necessary is to take some standard red thing and have a relation which one might call 'colour-likeness', sameness of colour, which would be a direct relation, not consisting in having a certain colour. You can then define the things which are red, as all the things that have colour-likeness to this standard thing. That is practically the treatment that Berkeley and Hume recommended, except that they did not recognize that they were reducing qualities to relations, but thought they were getting rid of 'abstract ideas' altogether. You can perfectly well do in that way a formal reduction of predicates to relations. There is no objection to that either empirically or logically. If you think it is worth while you can proceed in exactly the same way with dyadic relations, which you can reduce to triadic. Royce used to have a great affection for that process. For some reason he always liked triadic relations better than dyadic ones; he illustrated his preference in his contributions to mathematical logic and the principles of geometry.

All that is possible. I do not myself see any particular point in doing it as soon as you have realized that it is possible. I see no particular reason to suppose that the simplest relations that occur in the world are (say) of order *n*, but there is no *a priori* reason against it. The converse reduction, on the other hand, is quite impossible except in certain special cases where the relation has some special properties. For example, dyadic relations can be reduced to sameness of predicate when they are symmetrical and transitive. Thus, e.g. the relation of colour-likeness will have the property that if *A* has exact colour-likeness with *B* and *B* with *C*, then *A* has exact colour-likeness with *C*; and if *A* has it with *B*, *B* has it with *A*. But the case is otherwise with asymmetrical relations.

Take for example '*A* is greater than *B*'. It is obvious that '*A* is greater than *B*' does not consist in *A* and *B* having a common predicate, for if it did it would require that *B* should also be greater than *A*. It is also obvious that it does not consist merely in their having different predicates, because if *A* has a different predicate from *B*, *B* has a different predicate from *A*, so that in either case, whether of sameness or difference of predicate, you get a symmetrical relation. For instance, if *A* is of a different colour from *B*, *B* is of a different colour from *A*. Therefore when you get symmetrical relations, you have relations which it is formally possible to reduce to either sameness of predicate or difference of predicate, but when you come to asymmetrical relations there is no such possibility. This impossibility of reducing dyadic relations to sameness or difference of predicate is a matter of a good deal of importance in connection with traditional philosophy, because a great deal of traditional philosophy depends upon the assumption that every proposition really is of the subject-predicate form, and that is certainly not the case. That theory dominates a great part of traditional metaphysics and the old idea of substance and a good deal of the theory of the

Absolute, so that that sort of logical outlook which had its imagination dominated by the theory that you could always express a proposition in a subject-predicate form has had a very great deal of influence upon traditional metaphysics.

That is the end of what I ought to have said last time, and I come on now to the proper topic of today's lecture, that is *molecular* propositions. I call them molecular propositions because they contain other propositions which you may call their atoms, and by molecular propositions I mean propositions having such words as 'or', 'if', 'and', and so forth. If I say, 'Either today is Tuesday, or we have all made a mistake in being here', that is the sort of proposition that I mean that is molecular. Or if I say, 'If it rains, I shall bring my umbrella', that again is a molecular proposition because it contains the two parts 'It rains' and 'I shall bring my umbrella'. If I say, 'It did rain and I did bring my umbrella', that again is a molecular proposition. Or if I say, 'The supposition of its raining is incompatible with the supposition of my not bringing my umbrella', that again is a molecular proposition. There are various propositions of that sort, which you can complicate *ad infinitum*. They are built up out of propositions related by such words as 'or', 'if', 'and', and so on. You remember that I defined an atomic proposition as one which contains a single verb. Now there are two different lines of complication in proceeding from these to more complex propositions. There is the line that I have just been talking about, where you proceed to molecular propositions, and there is another line which I shall come to in a later lecture, where you have not two related propositions, but one proposition containing two or more verbs. Examples are got from believing, wishing, and so forth. 'I believe Socrates is mortal.' You have there two verbs, 'believe' and 'is'. Or 'I wish I were immortal'. Anything like that where you have a wish or a belief or a doubt involves two verbs. A lot of psychological attitudes involve two verbs, not, as it were, crystallized out, but two verbs within the one unitary proposition. But I am talking today about molecular propositions and you will understand that you can make propositions with 'or' and 'and' and so forth, where the constituent propositions are not atomic, but for the moment we can confine ourselves to the case where the constituent propositions are atomic. When you take an atomic proposition, or one of these propositions like 'believing', when you take any proposition of that sort, there is just one fact which is pointed to by the proposition, pointed to either truly or falsely. The essence of a proposition is that it can correspond in two ways with a fact, in what one may call the true way or the false way. You might illustrate it in a picture like this:

True:      $\overrightarrow{\text{Prop. Fact}}$

False:      $\text{Fact } \overrightarrow{\text{Prop.}}$

Supposing you have the proposition 'Socrates is mortal', either there would be the fact that Socrates is mortal or there would be the fact that Socrates is not mortal. In the one case it corresponds in a way that makes the proposition true, in the other case in a way that makes the proposition false. That is one way in which a proposition differs from a name.

There are, of course, two propositions corresponding to every fact, one true and one false. There are no false facts, so you cannot get one fact for every proposition but only for every pair of propositions. All that applies to atomic propositions. But when you take such a proposition as '$p$ or $q$', 'Socrates is mortal or Socrates is living still', there you will have two different facts involved in the truth or the falsehood of your proposition '$p$ or $q$'. There will be the fact that corresponds to $p$ and there will be the fact that corresponds to $q$, and both of those facts are relevant in discovering the truth or falsehood of '$p$ or $q$'. I do not suppose there is in the world a single disjunctive fact corresponding to '$p$ or $q$'. It does not look plausible that in the actual objective world there are facts going about which

you could describe as '$p$ or $q$', but I would not lay too much
stress on what strikes one as plausible: it is not a thing you
can rely on altogether. For the present I do not think any
difficulties will arise from the supposition that the truth or
falsehood of this proposition '$p$ or $q$' does not depend upon
a single objective fact which is disjunctive but depends on
the two facts one of which corresponds to $p$ and the other
to $q$: $p$ will have a fact corresponding to it and $q$ will have
a fact corresponding it. That is to say, the truth or falsehood of this proposition '$p$ or $q$' depends upon two facts
and not upon one, as $p$ does and as $q$ does. Generally
speaking, as regards these things that you make up out of
two propositions, the whole of what is necessary in order
to know their meaning is to know under what circum-
stances they are true, given the truth or falsehood of $p$ and
the truth or falsehood of $q$. That is perfectly obvious. You
have as a schema, for '$p$ or $q$', using

'$TT$' for '$p$ and $q$ both true'
'$TF$' for '$p$ true and $q$ false', etc.

| $TT$ | $TF$ | $FT$ | $FF$ |
|------|------|------|------|
| $T$  | $T$  | $T$  | $F$  |

where the bottom line states the truth or the falsehood of
'$p$ or $q$'. You must not look about the real world for an
object which you can call 'or', and say, 'Now, look at this.
This is "or".' There is no such thing, and if you try to
analyse '$p$ or $q$' in that way you will get into trouble. But
the meaning of disjunction will be entirely explained by
the above schema.

I call these things truth-functions of propositions, when
the truth or falsehood of the molecular proposition depends only on the truth or falsehood of the propositions
that enter into it. The same applies to '$p$ and $q$' and 'if $p$
then $q$' and '$p$ is incompatible with $q$'. When I say '$p$ is
incompatible with $q$' I simply mean to say that they are not
both true. I do not mean any more. Those sorts of things
are called truth-functions, and these molecular proposi-

tions that we are dealing with today are instances of truth-functions. If $p$ is a proposition, the statement that 'I believe $p$' does not depend for its truth or falsehood, simply upon the truth or falsehood of $p$, since I believe some but not all true propositions and some but not all false propositions.

I just want to give you a little talk about the way these truth-functions are built up. You can build up all these different sorts of truth-functions out of one source, namely '$p$ is incompatible with $q$', meaning by that that they are not both true, that one at least of them is false.

We will denote '$p$ is incompatible with $q$' by $p/q$.

Take for instance $p$-$p$, i.e. '$p$ is incompatible with itself'. In that case clearly $p$ will be false, so that you can take '$p/p$' as meaning '$p$ is false', i.e. $p/p$=not $p$. The meaning of molecular propositions is entirely determined by their truth-schema and there is nothing more in it than that, so that when you have got two things of the same truth-schema you can identify them.

Suppose you want 'if $p$ then $q$', that simply means that you cannot have $p$ without having $q$, so that $p$ is incompatible with the falsehood of $q$. Thus,

'If $p$ then $q$'$=p/(q/q)$.

When you have that, it follows of course at once that if $p$ is true, $q$ is true, because you cannot have $p$ true and $q$ false.

Suppose you want '$p$ or $q$', that means that the falsehood of $p$ is incompatible with the falsehood of $q$. If $p$ is false, $q$ is not false, and vice versa. That will be:

$(p/p)/(q/q)$.

Suppose you want '$p$ and $q$ are both true'. That will mean that $p$ is not incompatible with $q$. When $p$ and $q$ are both true, it is not the case that at least one of them is false. Thus,

'$p$ and $q$ are both true'$=(p/q)/(p/q)$.

The whole of the logic of deduction is concerned simply with complications and developments of this idea. This idea of incompatibility was first shown to be sufficient for the purpose by Mr. Sheffer, and there was a good deal of work done subsequently by M. Nicod. It is a good deal simpler when it is done this way than when it is done in the way of *Principia Mathematica,* where there are two primitive ideas to start with, namely 'or' and 'not'. Here you can get on with only a single premiss for deduction. I will not develop this subject further because it takes you right into mathematical logic.

I do not see any reason to suppose that there is a complexity in the facts corresponding to these molecular propositions, because, as I was saying, the correspondence of a molecular proposition with facts is of a different sort from the correspondence of an atomic proposition with a fact. There is one special point that has to be gone into in connection with this, that is the question: Are there negative facts? Are there such facts as you might call the fact that 'Socrates is not alive'? I have assumed in all that I have said hitherto that there are negative facts, that for example if you say 'Socrates is alive', there is corresponding to that proposition in the real world the fact that Socrates is not alive. One has a certain repugnance to negative facts, the same sort of feeling that makes you wish not to have a fact '*p* or *q*' going about the world. You have a feeling that there are only positive facts, and that negative propositions have somehow or other got to be expressions of positive facts. When I was lecturing on this subject at Harvard[4] I argued that there were negative facts, and it nearly produced a riot: the class would not hear of there being negative facts at all. I am still inclined to think that there are. However, one of the men to whom I was lecturing at Harvard, Mr. Demos, subsequently wrote an article in *Mind* to explain why there are no negative facts. It is in *Mind* for April 1917. I think he makes as good a case as can be made for the view that there are no negative facts. It is a difficult question. I

---

[4][In 1914.]

really only ask that you should not dogmatize. I do not say positively that there are, but there may be.

There are certain things you can notice about negative propositions. Mr. Demos points out, *first* of all, that a negative proposition is not in any way dependent on a cognitive subject for its definition. To this I agree. Suppose you say, when I say 'Socrates is not alive', I am merely expressing disbelief in the proposition that Socrates is alive. You have got to find something or other in the real world to make this disbelief true, and the only question is what. That is his *first* point.

His *second* is that a negative proposition must not be taken as its face value. You cannot, he says, regard the statement 'Socrates is not alive' as being an expression of a fact in the same sort of direct way in which 'Socrates is human' would be an expression of a fact. His argument for that is solely that he cannot believe that there are negative facts in the world. He maintains that there cannot be in the real world such facts as 'Socrates is not alive', taken, i.e. as simple facts, and that therefore you have got to find some explanation of negative propositions, some interpretation, and that they cannot be just as simple as positive propositions. I shall come back to that point, but on this I do not feel inclined to agree.

His *third* point I do not entirely agree with: that when the word 'not' occurs, it cannot be taken as a qualification of the predicate. For instance, if you say that 'This is not red', you might attempt to say that 'not-red' is a predicate, but that of course won't do; in the first place because a great many propositions are not expressions of predicates; in the second place because the word 'not' applies to the whole proposition. The proper expression would be 'not: this is red'; the 'not' applies to the whole proposition 'this is red', and of course in many cases you can see that quite clearly. If you take a case I took in discussing descriptions: 'The present king of France is not bald', and if you take 'not-bald' as a predicate, that would have to be judged false on the ground that there is not a present king of France.

But it is clear that the proposition 'The present king of France is bald' is a false proposition, and therefore the negative of that will have to be a true proposition, and that could not be the case if you take 'not-bald' as a predicate, so that in all cases where a 'not' comes in, the 'not' has to be taken to apply to the whole proposition. 'Not $p$' is the proper formula.

We have come now to the question, how are we really to interpret 'not-$p$', and the suggestion offered by Mr. Demos is that when we assert 'not-$p$' we are really asserting that there is some proposition $q$ which is true and is incompatible with $p$ ('an opposite of $p$' is his phrase, but I think the meaning is the same). That is his suggested definition:

> 'not-$p$' means 'There is a proposition $q$ which is true and is incompatible with $p$.'

As, e.g., if I say 'This chalk is not red', I shall be meaning to assert that there is some proposition, which in this case would be the proposition 'This chalk is white', which is inconsistent with the proposition 'It is red', and that you use these general negative forms because you do not happen to know what the actual proposition is that is true and is incompatible with $p$. Or, of course, you may possibly know what the actual proposition is, but you may be more interested in the fact that $p$ is false than you are in the particular example which makes it false. As, for instance, you might be anxious to prove that someone is a liar, and you might be very much interested in the falsehood of some proposition which he had asserted. You might also be more interested in the general proposition than in the particular case, so that if someone had asserted that that chalk was red, you might be more interested in the fact that it was not red than in the fact that it was white.

I find it very difficult to believe that theory of falsehood. You will observe that in the first place there is this objection, that it makes incompatibility fundamental and an objective fact, which is not so very much simpler than allowing negative facts. You have got to have here 'That

$p$ is incompatible with $q$' in order to reduce 'not' to incompatibility, because this has got to be the corresponding fact. It is perfectly clear, whatever may be the interpretation of 'not', that there is *some* interpretation which will give you a fact. If I say 'There is not a hippopotamus in this room', it is quite clear there is some way of interpreting that statement according to which there is a corresponding fact, and the fact cannot be merely that every part of this room is filled up with something that is not a hippopotamus. You would come back to the necessity for some kind or other fact of the sort that we have been trying to avoid. We have been trying to avoid both negative facts and molecular facts, and all that this succeeds in doing is to substitute molecular facts for negative facts, and I do not consider that that is very successful as a means of avoiding paradox, especially when you consider this, that even if incompatibility is to be taken as a sort of fundamental expression of fact, incompatibility is not between facts but between propositions. If I say '$p$ is incompatible with $q$', one at least of $p$ and $q$ has got to be false. It is clear that no two *facts* are incompatible. The incompatibility holds *between the propositions,* between the $p$ and the $q$, and therefore if you are going to take incompatibility as a fundamental fact, you have got, in explaining negatives, to take as your fundamental fact something involving propositions as opposed to facts. It is quite clear that propositions are not what you might call 'real'. If you were making an inventory of the world, propositions would not come in. Facts would, beliefs, wishes, wills would, but propositions would not. They do not have being independently, so that this incompatibility of propositions taken as an ultimate fact of the real world will want a great deal of treatment, a lot of dressing up before it will do. Therefore as a simplification to avoid negative facts, I do not think it really is very successful. I think you will find that it is simpler to take negative facts as facts, to assume that 'Socrates is not alive' is really an objective fact in the same sense in which 'Socrates is human' is a fact. This theory of Mr. Demos's that I have been setting forth here is a development of the one one hits upon at once when one tries to get round negative facts, but for the reasons that I have given, I do not think it really answers to take things that way, and I think you will find that it is better to take negative facts as ultimate. Otherwise you will find it so difficult to say what it is that corresponds to a proposition. When, e.g. you have a false positive proposition, say 'Socrates is alive', it is false because of a fact in the real world. A thing cannot be false except because of a fact, so that you find it extremely difficult to say what exactly happens when you make a positive assertion that is false, unless you are going to admit negative facts. I think all those questions are difficult and there are arguments always to be adduced both ways, but on the whole I do incline to believe that there are negative facts and that there are not disjunctive facts. But the denial of disjunctive facts leads to certain difficulties which we shall have to consider in connection with general propositions in a later lecture.

*Discussion*

*Question:* Do you consider that the proposition 'Socrates is dead' is a positive or a negative fact?

*Mr. Russell:* It is partly a negative fact. To say that a person is dead is complicated. It is two statements rolled into one: 'Socrates was alive' and 'Socrates is not alive'.

*Question:* Does putting the 'not' into it give it a formal character of negative and vice versa?

*Mr. Russell:* No, I think you must go into the meaning of words.

*Question:* I should have thought there was a great difference between saying that 'Socrates is alive' and saying that 'Socrates is not a living man'. I think it is possible to have what one might call a negative existence and that things exist of which we cannot take cognizance. Socrates undoubtedly does live but he is no longer in the condition of living as a man.

*Mr. Russell:* I was not going into the question of existence after death but simply taking words in their everyday signification.

*Question:* What is precisely your test as to whether you have got a positive or negative proposition before you?

*Mr. Russell:* There is no formal test.

*Question:* If you had a formal test, would it not follow that you would know whether there were negative facts or not?

*Mr. Russell:* No, I think not. In the perfect logical language that I sketched in theory, it would always be obvious at once whether a proposition was positive or negative. But it would not bear upon how you are going to interpret negative propositions.

*Question:* Would the existence of negative facts ever be anything more than a mere definition?

*Mr. Russell:* Yes, I think it would. It seems to me that the business of metaphysics is to describe the world, and it is in my opinion a real definite question whether in a complete description of the world you would have to mention negative facts or not.

*Question:* How do you define a negative fact?

*Mr. Russell:* You could not give a general definition if it is right that negativeness is an ultimate.

## IV. Propositions and Facts with More than One Verb: Beliefs, Etc.

You will remember that after speaking about atomic propositions I pointed out two more complicated forms of propositions which arise immediately on proceeding further than that: the *first,* which I call molecular propositions, which I dealt with last time, involving such words as 'or', 'and', 'if', and the *second* involving two or more verbs such as believing, wishing, willing, and so forth. In the case of molecular propositions it was not clear that we had to deal with any new form of fact, but only with a new form of proposition, i.e. if you have a disjunctive proposition such as '*p* or *q*' it does not seem very plausible to say that there is in the world a disjunctive fact corresponding to '*p* or *q*' but merely that there is a fact corresponding to *p* and a fact corresponding to *q*, and the disjunctive proposition derives its truth or falsehood from those two separate facts. Therefore in that case one was dealing only with a new form of proposition and not with a few form of fact. Today we have to deal with a new form of fact.

I think one might describe philosophical logic, the philosophical portion of logic which is the portion that I am concerned with in these lectures since Christmas (1917), as an inventory, or if you like a more humble word, a 'zoo' containing all the different forms that facts may have. I should prefer to say 'forms of facts' rather than 'forms of propositions'. To apply that to the case of molecular propositions which I dealt with last time, if one were pursuing this analysis of the forms of facts, it would be *belief in* a molecular proposition that one would deal with rather than the molecular proposition itself. In accordance with the sort of realistic bias that I should put into all study of metaphysics, I should always wish to be engaged in the investigation of some actual fact or set of facts, and it seems to me that that is so in logic just as much as it is in zoology. In logic you are concerned with the forms of facts, with getting hold of the different sorts of facts, different *logical* sorts of facts, that there are in the world. Now I want to point out today that the facts that occur when one believes or wishes or wills have a different logical form from the atomic facts containing a single verb which I dealt with in my second lecture. (There are, of course, a good many forms that facts may have, a strictly infinite number, and I do not wish you to suppose that I pretend to deal with all of them.) Suppose you take any actual occurrence of a belief. I want you to understand that I am not talking about beliefs in the sort of way in which judgment is spoken of in theory of knowledge, in which you would say there is *the* judgment that two and two are four. I am talking of the actual occurrence of a belief in a particular person's mind at a particular moment, and discussing what sort of a fact that is. If I say 'What day of the week is this?' and you say 'Tuesday', there occurs in your mind at that moment the belief that this is Tuesday. The thing I want to deal with today is the question: What is the form of the fact which occurs when a person has a belief? Of course you see that the sort of obvious first notion that one would naturally arrive at would be that a belief is a relation to the proposition. 'I believe the proposition $p$.' 'I believe that today is Tuesday.' 'I believe that two and two are four.' Something like that. It seems on the face of it as if you had there a relation of the believing subject to a proposition. That view won't do for various reasons which I shall go into. But you have, therefore, got to have a theory of belief which is not exactly that. Take any sort of proposition, say 'I believe Socrates is mortal'. Suppose that that belief does actually occur. The statement that it occurs is a statement of fact. You have there two verbs. You may have more than two verbs, you may have any number greater than one. I may believe that Jones is of the opinion that Socrates is mortal. There you have more than two verbs. You may have any number, but you cannot have less than two. You will perceive that it is not only the proposition that has the two verbs, but also the fact, which is expressed by the proposition, has two constituents corresponding to verbs. I shall call those constituents verbs for the sake of short-ness, as it is very difficult to find any word to describe all those objects which one denotes by verbs. Of course, that is strictly using the word 'verb' in two different senses, but I do not think it can lead to any confusion if you under-stand that it is being so used. This fact (the belief) is one fact. It is not like what you had in molecular propositions where you had (say) '$p$ or $q$'. It is just one single fact that you have a belief. That is obvious from the fact that you can believe a falsehood. It is obvious from the fact of false belief that you cannot cut off one part: you cannot have

I believe/Socrates is mortal.

There are certain questions that arise about such facts, and the first that arises is, Are they undeniable facts or can you reduce them in some way to relations of other facts? Is it really necessary to suppose that there are irreducible facts, of which that sort of thing is a verbal expression? On that question until fairly lately I should certainly not have supposed that any doubt could arise. It had not really seemed to me until fairly lately that that was a debatable point. I still believe that there are facts of that form, but I see that it is a substantial question that needs to be discussed.

### 1. Are beliefs, etc., irreducible facts?

'Etc.' covers understanding a proposition; it covers desiring, willing, any other attitude of that sort that you may think of that involves a proposition. It seems natural to say one believes a proposition and unnatural to say one desires a proposition, but as a matter of fact that is only a prejudice. What you believe and what you desire are of exactly the same nature. You may desire to get some sugar tomorrow and of course you may possibly believe that you will. I am not sure that the logical form is the same in the case of will. I am inclined to think that the case of will is more analogous to that of perception, in going direct to facts, and excluding the possibility of falsehood. In any case desire and belief are of exactly the same form logically.

Pragmatists and some of the American realists, the school whom one calls neutral monists, deny altogether that there is such a phenomenon as belief in the sense I am dealing with. They do not deny it in words, they do not use the same sort of language that I am using, and that makes it difficult to compare their views with the views I am speaking about. One has really to translate what they say into language more or less analogous to ours before one can make out where the points of contact or difference are. If you take the works of James in his *Essays in Radical Empiricism* or Dewey in his *Essays in Experimental Logic* you will find that they are denying altogether that there is such a phenomenon as belief in the sense I am talking of. They use the word 'believe' but they mean something different.

You come to the view called 'behaviourism', according to which you mean, if you say a person believes a thing, that he behaves in a certain fashion; and that hangs together with James's pragmatism. James and Dewey would say: when I believe a proposition, that *means* that I act in a certain fashion, that my behaviour has certain characteristics, and my belief is a true one if the behaviour leads to the desired result and is a false one if it does not. That, if it is true, makes their pragmatism a perfectly rational account of truth and falsehood, if you do accept their view that belief as an isolated phenomenon does not occur. That is therefore the first thing one has to consider. It would take me too far from logic to consider that subject as it deserves to be considered, because it is a subject belonging to psychology, and it is only relevant to logic in this one way that it raises a doubt whether there are any facts having the logical form that I am speaking of. In the question of this logical form that involves two or more verbs you have a curious interlacing of logic with empirical studies, and of course that may occur elsewhere, in this way, that an empirical study gives you an example of a thing having a certain logical form, and you cannot really be sure that there are things having a given logical form except by finding an example, and the finding of an example is itself empirical. Therefore in that way empirical facts are relevant to logic at certain points. I think theoretically one might know that there were those forms without knowing any instance of them, but practically, situated as we are, that does not seem to occur. Practically, unless you can find an example of the form you won't know that there is that form. If I cannot find an example containing two or more verbs, you will not have reason to believe in the theory that such a form occurs.

When you read the words of people like James and Dewey on the subject of belief, one thing that strikes you at once is that the sort of thing they are thinking of as the object of belief is quite different from the sort of thing I am thinking of. They think of it always as a thing. They think

you believe in God or Homer: you believe in an object.
That is the picture thay have in their minds. It is common
enough, in common parlance, to talk that way, and they
would say, the first crude approximation that they would
suggest would be that you believe truly when there is such
an object and that you believe falsely when there is not.
I do not mean they would say that exactly, but that would
be the crude view from which they would start. They do
not seem to have grasped the fact that the objective side
in belief is better expressed by a proposition than by a
single word, and that, I think, has a great deal to do with
their whole outlook on the matter of what belief consists
of. The object of belief in their view is generally, not relations between things, or things having qualities, or what
not, but just single things which may or may not exist.
That view seems to me radically and absolutely mistaken.
In the *first* place there are a great many judgments you
cannot possibly fit into that scheme, and in the *second* place
it cannot possibly give any explanation to false beliefs,
because when you believe that a thing exists and it does
not exist, the thing is not there, it is nothing, and it cannot
be the right analysis of a false belief to regard it as a
relation to what is really nothing. This is an objection to
supposing that belief consists simply in relation to the
object. It is obvious that if you say 'I believe in Homer' and
there was no such person as Homer, your belief cannot be
a relation to Homer, since there is no 'Homer'. Every fact
that occurs in the world must be composed entirely of
constituents that there are, and not of constituents that
there are not. Therefore when you say 'I believe in Homer'
it cannot be the right analysis of the thing to put it like that.
What the right analysis is I shall come on to in the theory
of descriptions. I come back now to the theory of behaviourism which I spoke of a moment ago. Suppose, e.g. that you
are said to believe that there is a train at 10.25. This means,
we are told, that you start for the station at a certain time.
When you reach the station you see it is 10.24 and you run.
That behaviour constitutes your belief that there is a train

at that time. If you catch your train by running, your belief was true. If the train went at 10.23, you miss it, and your belief was false. That is the sort of thing that they would say constitutes belief. There is not a single state of mind which consists in contemplating this eternal verity, that the train starts at 10.25. They would apply that even to the most abstract things. I do not myself feel that that view of things is tenable. It is a difficult one to refute because it goes very deep and one has the feeling that perhaps, if one thought it out long enough and became sufficiently aware of all its implications, one might find after all that it was a feasible view; but yet I do not *feel* it feasible. It hangs together, of course, with the theory of neutral monism, with the theory that the material constituting the mental is the same as the material constituting the physical, just like the Post Office directory which gives you people arranged geographically and alphabetically. This whole theory hangs together with that. I do not mean necessarily that all the people that profess the one profess the other, but that the two do essentially belong together. If you are going to take that view, you have to explain away belief and desire, because things of that sort do seem to be mental phenomena. They do seem rather far removed from the sort of thing that happens in the physical world. Therefore people will set to work to explain away such things as belief, and reduce them to bodily behaviour; and your belief in a certain proposition will consist in the behaviour of your body. In the crudest terms that is what that view amounts to. It does enable you to get on very well without mind. Truth and falsehood in that case consist in the relation of your bodily behaviour to a certain fact, the sort of distant fact which is the purpose of your behaviour, as it were, and when your behaviour is satisfactory in regard to that fact your belief is true, and when your behaviour is unsatisfactory in regard to that fact your belief is false. The logical essence, in that view, will be a relation between two facts having the same sort of form as a causal relation, i.e. on the one hand there will be your bodily behaviour which is one fact, and on the other hand the fact that the train starts at such and such a time, which is another fact, and out of a relation of those two the whole phenomenon is constituted. The thing you will get will be logically of the same form as you have in cause, where you have 'This fact causes that fact'. It is quite a different logical form from the facts containing two verbs that I am talking of today.

I have naturally a bias in favour of the theory of neutral monism because it exemplifies Occam's razor. I always wish to get on in philosophy with the smallest possible apparatus, partly because it diminishes the risk of error, because it is not necessary to deny the entities you do not assert, and therefore you run less risk of error the fewer entities you assume. The other reason—perhaps a some-what frivolous one—is that every diminution in the num-ber of entities increases the amount of work for mathematical logic to do in building up things that look like the entities you used to assume. Therefore the whole theory of neutral monism is pleasing to me, but I do find so far very great difficulty in believing it. You will find a discussion of the whole question in some articles I wrote in *The Monist*,[5] especially in July 1914, and in the two previous numbers also. I should really want to rewrite them rather because I think some of the arguments I used against neutral mon-ism are not valid. I place most reliance on the argument about 'emphatic particulars', 'this', 'I', all that class of words, that pick out certain particulars from the universe by their relation to oneself, and I think by the fact that they, or particulars related to them, are present to you at the mo-ment of speaking. 'This', of course, is what I call an 'em-phatic particular'. It is simply a proper name for the present object of attention, a proper name, meaning nothing. It is ambiguous, because, of course, the object of attention is

_____

[5][Reprinted as 'On the Nature of Acquaintance' in R. C. Marsh ed., *Logic and Knowledge*.]

always changing from moment to moment and from person to person. I think it is extremely difficult, if you get rid of consciousness altogether, to explain what you mean by such a word as 'this', what it is that makes the absence of impartiality. You would say that in a purely physical world there would be a complete impartiality. All parts of time and all regions of space would seem equally emphatic. But what really happens is that we pick out certain facts, past and future and all that sort of thing; they all radiate out from 'this', and I have not myself seen how one can deal with the notion of 'this' on the basis of neutral monism. I do not lay that down dogmatically, only I do not see how it can be done. I shall assume for the rest of this lecture that there are such facts as beliefs and wishes and so forth. It would take me really the whole of my course to go into the question fully. Thus we come back to more purely logical questions from this excursion into psychology, for which I apologize.

## 2. What is the status of p in 'I believe p'?

You cannot say that you believe *facts,* because your beliefs are sometimes wrong. You can say that you *perceive* facts, because perceiving is not liable to error. Wherever it is facts alone that are involved, error is impossible. Therefore you cannot say you believe facts. You have to say that you believe propositions. The awkwardness of that is that obviously propositions are nothing. Therefore that cannot be the true account of the matter. When I say 'Obviously propositions are nothing' it is not perhaps quite obvious. Time was when I thought there were propositions, but it does not seem to me very plausible to say that in addition to facts there are also these curious shadowy things going about such as 'That today is Wednesday' when in fact it is Tuesday. I cannot believe they go about the real world. It is more than one can manage to believe, and I do think no person with a vivid sense of reality can imagine it. One of the difficulties of the study of logic is that it is an exceedingly abstract study dealing with the most abstract things imaginable, and yet you cannot pursue it properly unless you have a vivid instinct as to what is real. You must have that instinct rather well developed in logic. I think otherwise you will get into fantastic things. I think Meinong is rather deficient in just that instinct for reality. Meinong maintains that there is such an object as the round square only it does not exist, and it does not even subsist, but nevertheless there is such an object, and when you say 'The round square is a fiction', he takes it that there is an object 'the round square' and there is a predicate 'fiction'. No one with a sense of reality would so analyse that proposition. He would see that the proposition wants analysing in such a way that you won't have to regard the round square as a constituent of that proposition. To suppose that in the actual world of nature there is a whole set of false propositions going about is to my mind monstrous. I cannot bring myself to suppose it. I cannot believe that they are there in the sense in which facts are there. There seems to me something about the fact that 'Today is Tuesday' on a different level of reality from the supposition 'That today is Wednesday'. When I speak of the proposition 'That today is Wednesday' I do not mean the occurrence in future of a state of mind in which you think it is Wednesday, but I am talking about the theory that there is something quite logical, something not involving mind in any way; and such a thing as that I do not think you can take a false proposition to be. I think a false proposition must, wherever it occurs, be subject to analysis, be taken to pieces, pulled to bits, and shown to be simply separate pieces of one fact in which the false proposition has been analysed away. I say that simply on the ground of what I should call an instinct of reality. I ought to say a word or two about 'reality'. It is a vague word, and most of its uses are improper. When I talk about reality as I am now doing, I can explain best what I mean by saying that I mean everything you would have to mention in a complete description of the world; that will convey to you what I mean. Now I do *not* think that false propositions would have to be mentioned in a complete description of the world. False beliefs would, of course, false suppositions would, and desires for what does not come to pass, but not false propositions all alone, and therefore when you, as one says, believe a false proposition, that cannot be an accurate account of what occurs. It is not accurate to say 'I believe the proposition $p$' and regard the occurrence as a twofold relation between me and $p$. The logical form is just the same whether you believe a false or a true proposition. Therefore in all cases you are not to regard belief as a two-term relation between yourself and a proposition, and you have to analyse up the proposition and treat your belief differently. Therefore the belief does not really contain a proposition as a constituent but only contains the constituents of the proposition as constituents. You cannot say when you believe, 'What is it that you believe?' There is no answer to that question, i.e. there is not a single thing that you are believing. 'I believe that today is Tuesday.' You must not suppose that 'That today is Tuesday' is a single object which I am believing. That would be an error. That is not the right way to analyse the occurrence, although that analysis is linguistically convenient, and one may keep it provided one knows that it is not the truth.

### 3. How shall we describe the logical form of a belief?

I want to try to get an account of the way that a belief is made up. That is not an easy question at all. You cannot make what I should call a map-in-space of a belief. You can make a map of an atomic fact but not of a belief, for the simple reason that space-relations always are of the atomic sort or complications of the atomic sort. I will try to illustrate what I mean. The point is in connection with there being two verbs in the judgment and with the fact that both verbs have got to occur as verbs, because if a thing is a verb it cannot occur otherwise than as a verb. Suppose I take 'A believes that B loves C'. 'Othello believes that Desdemona loves Cassio'. There you have a false belief. You have this odd state of affairs that the verb 'loves'

occurs in that proposition and seems to occur as relating
Desdemona to Cassio whereas in fact it does not do so, but
yet it does occur as a verb, it does occur in the sort of way
that a verb should do. I mean that when *A* believes that *B*
loves *C*, you have to have a verb in the place where 'loves'
occurs. You cannot put a substantive in its place. Therefore
it is clear that the subordinate verb (i.e. the verb other than
believing) is functioning as a verb, and seems to be relating
two terms, but as a matter of fact does not when a judgment happens to be false. That is what constitutes the
puzzle about the nature of belief. You will notice that wherever one gets to really close quarters with the theory of
error one has the puzzle of how to deal with error without
assuming the existence of the non-existent. I mean that
every theory of error sooner or later wrecks itself by assuming the existence of the non-existent. As when I say
'Desdemona loves Cassio', it seems as if you have a non-
existent love between Desdemona and Cassio, but that is
just as wrong as a non-existent unicorn. So you have to
explain the whole theory of judgment in some other way.
I come now to this question of a map. Suppose you try
such a map as this:

OTHELLO

beli ↓ eves

DESDEMONA ⟶ CASSIO

loves

This question of making a map is not so strange as you
might suppose because it is part of the whole theory of
symbolism. It is important to realize where and how a
symbolism of that sort would be wrong: where and how
it is wrong is that in the symbol you have this relationship
relating these two things and in the fact it doesn't really
relate them. You cannot get in space any occurrence which
is logically of the same form as belief. When I say 'logically
of the same form' I mean that one can be obtained from
the other by replacing the constituents of the one by the
new terms. If I say 'Desdemona loves Cassio' that is of the

same form as 'A is to the right of B'. Those are of the same form, and I say that nothing that occurs in space is of the same form as belief. I have got on here to a new sort of thing, a new beast for our zoo, not another member of our former species but a new species. The discovery of this fact is due to Mr. Wittgenstein.

There is a great deal that is odd about belief from a logical point of view. One of the things that are odd is that you can believe propositions of all sorts of forms. I can believe that 'This is white' and 'Two and two are four'. They are quite different forms, yet one can believe both. The actual occurrence can hardly be of exactly the same logical form in those two cases because of the great difference in the forms of the propositions believed. Therefore it would seem that belief cannot strictly be logically one in all different cases but must be distinguished according to the nature of the proposition that you believe. If you have 'I believe $p$' and 'I believe $q$' those two facts, if $p$ and $q$ are not of the same logical form, are not of the same logical form in the sense I was speaking of a moment ago, that is in the sense that from 'I believe $p$' you can derive 'I believe $q$' by replacing the constituents of one by the constituents of the other. That means that belief itself cannot be treated as being a proper sort of single term. Belief will really have to have different logical forms according to the nature of what is believed. So that the apparent sameness of believing in different cases is more or less illusory.

There are really two main things that one wants to notice in this matter that I am treating of just now. The *first* is the impossibility of treating the proposition believed as an independent entity, entering as a unit into the occurrence of the belief, and the *other* is the impossibility of putting the subordinate verb on a level with its terms as an object term in the belief. That is a point in which I think that the theory of judgment which I set forth once in print some years ago was a little unduly simple, because I did then treat the object verb as if one could put it as just an object like the terms, as if one could put 'loves' on a level with Desdemona and Cassio as a term for the relation 'believe'. That is why I have been laying such an emphasis on this lecture today on the fact that there are two verbs at least. I hope you will forgive the fact that so much of what I say today is tentative and consists of pointing out difficulties. The subject is not very easy and it has not been much dealt with or discussed. Practically nobody has until quite lately begun to consider the problem of the nature of belief with anything like a proper logical apparatus and therefore one has very little to help one in any discussion and so one has to be content on many points at present with pointing out difficulties rather than laying down quite clear solutions.

### 4. The question of nomenclature.

What sort of name shall we give to verbs like 'believe' and 'wish' and so forth? I should be inclined to call them 'propositional verbs'. This is merely a suggested name for convenience, because they are verbs which have the *form* of relating an object to a proposition. As I have been explaining, that is not what they really do, but it is convenient to call them propositional verbs. Of course you might call them 'attitudes', but I should not like that because it is a psychological term, and although all the instances in our experience are psychological, there is no reason to suppose that all the verbs I am talking of are psychological. There is never any reason to suppose that sort of thing. One should always remember Spinoza's infinite attributes of Deity. It is quite likely that there are in the world the analogues of his infinite attributes. We have no acquaintance with them, but there is no reason to suppose that the mental and the physical exhaust the whole universe, so one can never say that all the instances of any logical sort of thing are of such and such a nature which is not a logical nature: you do not know enough about the world for that. Therefore I should not suggest that all the verbs that have the form exemplified by believing and willing are psychological. I can only say all I know are.

I notice that in my syllabus I said I was going to deal with truth and falsehood today, but there is not much to say about them specifically as they are coming in all the time. The thing one first thinks of as true or false is a proposition, and a proposition is nothing. But a belief is true or false in the same way as a proposition is, so that you do have facts in the world that are true or false. I said a while back that there was no distinction of true and false among facts, but as regards that special class of facts that we call 'beliefs', there is, in that sense that a belief which occurs may be true or false, though it is equally a fact in either case. One *might* call wishes false in the same sense when one wishes something that does not happen. The truth or falsehood depends upon the proposition that enters in. I am inclined to think that perception, as opposed to belief, does go straight to the fact and not through the proposition. When you perceive the fact you do not, of course, have error coming in, because the moment it is a fact that is your object error is excluded. I think that verification in the last resort would always reduce itself to the perception of facts. Therefore the logical form of perception will be different from the logical form of believing, just because of that circumstance that it is a *fact* that comes in. That raises also a number of logical difficulties which I do not propose to go into, but I think you can see for yourself that perceiving would also involve two verbs just as believing does. I am inclined to think that volition differs from desire logically, in a way strictly analogous to that in which perception differs from belief. But it would take us too far from logic to discuss this view.

## V.  General Propositions and Existence

I am going to speak today about general propositions and existence. The two subjects really belong together; they are the same topic, although it might not have seemed so at the first glance. The propositions and facts that I have been talking about hitherto have all been such as involved only perfectly definite particulars, or relations, or qualities, or things of that sort, never involved the sort of indefinite things one alludes to by such words as 'all', 'some', 'a', 'any', and it is propositions and facts of that sort that I am coming on to today.

Really all the propositions of that sort that I mean to talk of today collect themselves into two groups—the *first* that are about 'all', and the *second* that are about 'some'. These two sorts belong together; they are each other's negations. If you say, for instance, 'All men are mortal', that is the negative of 'Some men are not mortal'. In regard to general propositions, the distinction of affirmative and negative is arbitrary. Whether you are going to regard the propositions about 'all' as the affirmative ones and the propositions about 'some' as the negative ones, or vice versa, is purely a matter of taste. For example, if I say 'I met no one as I came along', that, on the face of it, you would think is a negative proposition. Of course, that is really a proposition about 'all', i.e. 'All men are among those whom I did not meet'. If, on the other hand, I say 'I met a man as I came along', that would strike you as affirmative, whereas it is the negative of 'All men are among those I did not meet as I came along'. If you consider such propositions as 'All men are mortal' and 'Some men are not mortal', you might say it was more natural to take the general propositions as the affirmative and the existence-propositions as the negative, but, simply because it is quite arbitrary which one is to choose, it is better to forget these words and to speak only of general propositions and propositions asserting existence. All general propositions deny the existence of something or other. If you say 'All men are mortal', that denies the existence of an immortal man, and so on.

I want to say emphatically that general propositions are to be interpreted as not involving existence. When I say, for instance, 'All Greeks are men', I do not want you to suppose that that implies that there are Greeks. It is to be considered emphatically as not implying that. That would have to be added as a separate proposition. If you want to interpret it in that sense, you will have to add the further statement 'and there are Greeks'. That is for purposes of practical convenience. If you include the fact that there are Greeks, you are rolling two propositions into one, and it causes unnecessary confusion in your logic, because the sorts of propositions that you want are those that do assert the existence of something and general propositions which do not assert existence. If it happened that there were no Greeks, both the proposition that 'All Greeks are men' and the proposition that 'No Greeks are men' would be true. The proposition 'No Greeks are men' is, of course, the proposition 'All Greeks are not-men'. Both propositions will be true simultaneously if it happens that there are no Greeks. All statements about all the members of a class that has no members are true, because the contradictory of any general statement does assert existence and is therefore false in this case. This notion, of course, of general propositions not involving existence is one which is not in the traditional doctrine of the syllogism. In the traditional doctrine of the syllogism, it was assumed that when you have such a statement as 'All Greeks are men', that implies that there are Greeks, and this produced fallacies. For instance, 'All chimeras are animals, and all chimeras breathe flame, therefore some animals breathe flame.' This is a syllogism in Darapti, but that mood of the syllogism is fallacious, as this instance shows. That was a point, by the way, which had a certain historical interest, because it impeded Leibniz in his attempts to construct a mathematical logic. He was always engaged in trying to construct such a mathematical logic as we have now, or rather such a one as Boole constructed, and he was always failing because of his respect for Aristotle. Whenever he invented a really good system, as he did several times, it always brought out that such moods as Darapti are fallacious. If you say 'All $A$ is $B$ and all $A$ is $C$, therefore some $B$ is $C$'— if you say this you incur a fallacy, but he could not bring himself to believe that it was fallacious, so he began again.

That shows you that you should not have too much respect for distinguished men.[6]

Now when you come to ask what really is asserted in a general proposition, such as 'All Greeks are men' for instance, you find that what is asserted is the truth of all values of what I call a propositional function. A *propositional function* is simply *any expression containing an undetermined constituent, or several undetermined constituents, and becoming a proposition as soon as the undetermined constituents are determined.* If I say '*x* is a man' or '*n* is a number', that is a propositional function; so is any formula of algebra, say $(x+y)(x-y)=x^2-y^2$. A propositional function is nothing, but, like most of the things one wants to talk about in logic, it does not lose its importance through that fact. The only thing really that you can do with a propositional function is to assert either that it is always true, or that it is sometimes true, or that it is never true. If you take:

'If *x* is a man, *x* is mortal',

that is always true (just as much when *x* is not a man as when *x* is a man); if you take:

'*x* is a man',

that is sometimes true; if you take:

'*x* is a unicorn',

that is never true.

One may call a propositional function

*necessary,* when it is always true;
*possible,* when it is sometimes true;
*impossible,* when it is never true.

Much false philosophy has arisen out of confusing propositional functions and propositions. There is a great deal in ordinary traditional philosophy which consists simply in

---

[6]Cf. Couturat, *La logique de Leibniz.*

attributing to propositions the predicates which only apply to propositional functions, and, still worse, sometimes in attributing to individuals predicates which merely apply to propositional functions. This case of *necessary, possible, impossible,* is a case in point. In all traditional philosophy there comes a heading of 'modality', which discusses *necessary, possible,* and *impossible* as properties of propositions, whereas in fact they are properties of propositional functions. Propositions are only true or false.

If you take '*x* is *x*', that is a propositional function which is true whatever '*x*' may be, i.e. a necessary propositional function. If you take '*x* is a man', that is a possible one. If you take '*x* is a unicorn', that is an impossible one.

Propositions can only be true or false, but propositional functions have these three possibilities. It is important, I think, to realize that the whole doctrine of modality only applies to propositional functions, not to propositions.

Propositional functions are involved in ordinary language in a great many cases where one does not usually realize them. In such a statement as 'I met a man', you can understand my statement perfectly well without knowing whom I met, and the actual person is not a constituent of the proposition. You are really asserting there that a certain propositional function is sometimes true, namely the propositional function 'I met *x* and *x* is human'. There is at least one value of *x* for which that is true, and that therefore is a possible propositional function. Whenever you get such words as 'a', 'some', 'all', 'every', it is always a mark of the presence of a propositional function, so that these things are not, so to speak, remote or recondite: they are obvious and familiar.

A propositional function comes in again in such a statement as 'Socrates is mortal', because 'to be mortal' means 'to die at some time or other'. You mean there is a time at which Socrates dies, and that again involves a propositional function, namely that '*t* is a time, and Socrates dies at *t*' is possible. If you say 'Socrates is immortal', that also will involve a propositional function. That means that 'If

$t$ is any time whatever, Socrates is alive at time $t$', if we take immortality as involving existence throughout the whole of the past as well as throughout the whole of the future. But if we take immortality as only involving existence throughout the whole of the future, the interpretation of 'Socrates is immortal' becomes more complete, viz., 'There is a time $t$, such that if $t'$ is any time later than $t$, Socrates is alive at $t'$.' Thus when you come to write out properly what one means by a great many ordinary statements, it turns out a little complicated. 'Socrates is mortal' and 'Socrates is immortal' are not each other's contradictories, because they both imply that Socrates exists in time, otherwise he would not be either mortal or immortal. One says, 'There is a time at which he dies', and the other says, 'Whatever time you take, he is alive at that time', whereas the contradictory of 'Socrates is mortal' would be true if there is not a time at which he lives.

An undetermined constituent in a propositional function is called a *variable*.

*Existence.* When you take any propositional function and assert of it that it is possible, that it is sometimes true, that gives you the fundamental meaning of 'existence'. You may express it by saying that there is at least one value of $x$ for which that propositional function is true. Take '$x$ is a man', there is at least one value of $x$ for which this is true. That is what one means by saying that 'There are men', or that 'Men exist'. Existence is essentially a property of a propositional function. It means that that propositional function is true in at least one instance. If you say 'There are unicorns', that will mean that 'There is an $x$, such that $x$ is a unicorn'. That is written in phrasing which is unduly approximated to ordinary language, but the proper way to put it would be '($x$ is a unicorn) is possible'. We have got to have some idea that we do not define, and one takes the idea of 'always true', or of 'sometimes true', as one's undefined idea in this matter, and then you can define the other one as the negative of that. In some ways it is better to take them both as undefined, for reasons which I shall not go into at present. It will be out of this notion of *sometimes,* which is the same as the notion of *possible,* that we get the notion of existence. To say that unicorns exist is simply to say that '($x$ is a unicorn) is possible'.

It is perfectly clear that when you say 'Unicorns exist', you are not saying anything that would apply to any uni-corns there might happen to be, because as a matter of fact there are not any, and therefore if what you say had any application to the actual individuals, it could not possibly be significant unless it were true. You can consider the proposition 'Unicorns exist' and can see that it is false. It is not nonsense. Of course, if the proposition went through the general conception of the unicorn to the individual, it could not be even significant unless there were unicorns. Therefore when you say 'Unicorns exist', you are not say-ing anything about any individual things, and the same applies when you say 'Men exist'. If you say that 'Men exist, and Socrates is a man, therefore Socrates exists', that is exactly the same sort of fallacy as it would be if you said 'Men are numerous, Socrates is a man, therefore Socrates is numerous', because existence is a predicate of a proposi-tional function, or derivatively of a class. When you say of a propositional function that it is numerous, you will mean that there are several values of $x$ that will satisfy it, that there are more than one; or, if you like to take 'numerous' in a larger sense, more than ten, more than twenty, or whatever number you think fitting. If $x$, $y$, and $z$ all satisfy a propositional function, you may say that that proposition is numerous, but $x$, $y$, and $z$ severally are not numerous. Exactly the same applies to existence, that is to say that the actual things that there are in the world do not exist, or, at least, that is putting it too strongly, because that is utter nonsense. To say that they do not exist is strictly nonsense, but to say that they do exist is also strictly nonsense.

It is of propositional functions that you can assert or deny existence. You must not run away with the idea that this entails consequences that it does not entail. If I say 'The things that there are in the world exist', that is a perfectly correct statement, because I am there saying something about a certain class of things; I say it in the same sense in which I say 'Men exist'. But I must go on to 'This is a thing in the world, and therefore this exists'. It is there the fallacy comes in, and it is simply, as you see, a fallacy of transferring to the individual that satisfies a propositional function a predicate which only applies to a propositional function. You can see this in various ways. For instance, you sometimes know the truth of an existence-proposition without knowing any instance of it. You know that there are people in Timbuctoo, but I doubt if any of you could give me an instance of one. Therefore you clearly can know existence-propositions without knowing any individual that makes them true. Existence-propositions do not say anything about the actual individual but only about the class or function.

It is exceedingly difficult to make this point clear as long as one adheres to ordinary language, because ordinary language is rooted in a certain feeling about logic, a certain feeling that our primeval ancestors had, and as long as you keep to ordinary language you find it very difficult to get away from the bias which is imposed upon you by language. When I say, e.g. 'There is an $x$ such that $x$ is a man', that is not the sort of phrase one would like to use. 'There is an $x$' is meaningless. What is 'an $x$' anyhow? There is not such a thing. The only way you can really state it correctly is by inventing a new language *ad hoc*, and making the statement apply straight off to '$x$ is a man', as when one says '($x$ is a man) is possible', or invent a special symbol for the statement that '$x$ is a man' is sometimes true.

I have dwelt on this point because it really is of very fundamental importance. I shall come back to existence in my next lecture: existence as it applies to descriptions, which is a slightly more complicated case than I am discussing here. I think an almost unbelievable amount of false philosophy has arisen through not realizing what 'existence' means.

As I was saying a moment ago, a propositional function in itself is nothing: it is merely a schema. Therefore in the inventory of the world, which is what I am trying to get at, one comes to the question: What is there really in the world that corresponds with these things? Of course, it is clear that we have general *propositions,* in the same sense in which we have atomic propositions. For the moment I will include existence-propositions with general propositions. We have such propositions as 'All men are mortal' and 'Some men are Greeks'. But you have not only such *propositions;* you have also such *facts,* and that, of course, is where you get back to the inventory of the world: that, in addition to particular facts, which I have been talking about in previous lectures, there are also general facts and existence-facts, that is to say, there are not merely *propositions* of that sort but also *facts* of that sort. That is rather an important point to realize. You cannot ever arrive at a general fact by inference from particular facts, however numerous. The old plan of complete induction, which used to occur in books, which was always supposed to be quite safe and easy as opposed to ordinary induction, that plan of complete induction, unless it is accompanied by at least one general proposition, will not yield you the result that you want. Suppose, for example, that you wish to prove in that way that 'All men are mortal', you are supposed to proceed by complete induction, and say '$A$ is a man that is mortal', '$B$ is a man that is mortal', $C$ is a man that is mortal', and so on until you finish. You will not be able, in that way, to arrive at the proposition 'All men are mortal' unless you know when you have finished. That is to say that, in order to arrive by this road at the general proposition 'All men are mortal', you must already have the general proposition 'All men are among those I have enumerated'. You never can arrive at a general proposition by inference from particular propositions alone. You will always have to have at least one general proposition in your premises. That illustrates, I think, various points. One, which is epistemological, is that if there is, as there seems to be, knowledge of general propositions, then there must be *primitive* knowledge of general propositions (I mean by that, knowledge of general propositions which is not obtained by inference), because if you can never infer a general proposition except from premises of which one at least is general, it is clear that you can never have knowledge of such propositions by inference unless there is knowledge of some general propositions which is not by inference. I think that the sort of way such knowledge—or rather the belief that we have such knowledge—comes into ordinary life is probably very odd. I mean to say that we do habitually assume general propositions which are exceedingly doubtful; as, for instance, one might, if one were counting up the people in this room, assume that one could see all of them, which is a general proposition, and very doubtful as there may be people under the tables. But, apart from that sort of thing, you do have in any empirical verification of general propositions some kind of assumption that amounts to this, that what you do not see is not there. Of course, you would not put it so strongly as that, but you would assume that, with certain limitations and certain qualifications, if a thing does not appear to your senses, it is not there. That is a general proposition, and it is only through such propositions that you arrive at the ordinary empirical results that one obtains in ordinary ways. If you take census of the country, for instance, you assume that the people you do not see are not there, provided you search properly and carefully, otherwise your census might be wrong. It is some assumption of that sort which would underlie what seems purely empirical. You could not prove empirically that what you do not perceive is not there, because an empirical proof would consist in perceiving, and by hypothesis you do not perceive it, so that any proposition of that sort, if it is accepted, has to be accepted on its own evidence. I only take that as an illustra-tion. There are many other illustrations one could take of the sort of propositions that are commonly assumed, many of them with very little justification.

I come now to a question which concerns logic more nearly, namely, the reasons for supposing that there are general facts as well as general propositions. When we were discussing molecular propositions I threw doubt upon the supposition that there are molecular facts, but I do not think one can doubt that there are general facts. It is perfectly clear, I think, that when you have enumerated all the atomic facts in the world, it is a further fact about the world that those are all the atomic facts there are about the world, and that is just as much an objective fact about the world as any of them are. It is clear, I think, that you must admit general facts as distinct from and over and above particular facts. The same thing applies to 'All men are mortal'. When you have taken all the particular men that there are, and found each one of them severally to be mortal, it is definitely a new fact that all men are mortal; how new a fact, appears from what I said a moment ago, that it could not be inferred from the mortality of the several men that there are in the world. Of course, it is not so difficult to admit what I might call existence-facts—such facts as 'There are men', 'There are sheep', and so on. Those, I think, you will readily admit as separate and distinct facts over and above the atomic facts I spoke of before. Those facts have got to come into the inventory of the world, and in that way propositional functions come in as involved in the study of general facts. I do not profess to know what the right analysis of general facts is. It is an exceedingly difficult question, and one which I should very much like to see studied. I am sure that, although the convenient technical treatment is by means of propositional functions, that is not the whole of the right analysis. Beyond that I cannot go.

There is one point about whether there are molecular facts. I think I mentioned, when I was saying that I did not think there were disjunctive facts, that a certain difficulty does arise in regard to general facts. Take 'All men are mortal'. That means:

> ' "*x* is a man" implies
> "*x* is a mortal" whatever
> *x* may be.'

You see at once that it is a hypothetical proposition. It does not imply that there are any men, nor who are men, and who are not; it simply says that if you have anything which is a man, that thing is mortal. As Mr. Bradley has pointed out in the second chapter of his *Principles of Logic,* 'Trespassers will be prosecuted' may be true even if no one trespasses, since it means merely that, *if* any one trespasses, he will be prosecuted. It comes down to this that

> ' "*x* is a man" implies "*x* is a mortal" is always true',

is a fact. It is perhaps a little difficult to see how that can be true if one is going to say that ' "Socrates is a man" implies "Socrates is a mortal" ' is not itself a fact, which is what I suggested when I was discussing disjunctive facts. I do not feel sure that you could not get round that difficulty. I only suggest it as a point which should be considered when one is denying that there are molecular facts, since, if it cannot be got round, we shall have to admit molecular facts.

Now I want to come to the subject of *completely general* propositions and propositional functions. By those I mean propositions and propositional functions that contain only variables and nothing else at all. This covers the whole of logic. Every logical proposition consists wholly and solely of variables, though it is not true that every proposition consisting wholly and solely of variables is logical. You can consider stages of generalizations as, e.g.

> 'Socrates loves Plato'
> '*x* loves Plato'
> '*x* loves *y*'
> '*xRy*.'

There you have been going through a process of successive generalization. When you have got to *xRy*, you have got a schema consisting only of variables, containing no constants at all, the pure schema of dual relations, and it is clear that any proposition which expresses a dual relation can be derived from $xRy$ by assigning values to $x$ and $R$ and $y$. So that that is, as you might say, the pure form of all those propositions. I mean by the form of a proposition that which you get when for every single one of its constituents you substitute a variable. If you want a different definition of the form of a proposition, you might be inclined to define it as the class of all those propositions that you can obtain from a given one by substituting other constituents for one or more of the constituents the proposition contains. E.g. in 'Socrates loves Plato', you can substitute somebody else for Socrates, somebody else for Plato, and some other verb for 'loves'. In that way there are a certain number of propositions which you can derive from the proposition 'Socrates loves Plato', by replacing the constituents of that proposition by other constituents, so that you have there a certain class of propositions, and those propositions all have a certain form, and one can, if one likes, say that the form they all have is the class consisting of all of them. That is rather a provisional definition, because as a matter of fact, the idea of form is more fundamental than the idea of class. I should not suggest that as a really good definition, but it will do provisionally to explain the sort of thing one means by the form of a proposition. The form of a proposition is that which is in common between any two propositions of which the one can be obtained from the other by substituting other constituents for the original ones. When you have got down to those formulas that contain only variables, like $xRy$, you are on the way to the sort of thing that you can assert in logic.

To give an illustration, you know what I mean by the domain of a relation: I mean all the terms that have that relation to something. Suppose I say: '$xRy$ implies that $x$ belongs to the domain of $R$', that would be a proposition of logic and is one that contains only variables. You might think it contains such words as 'belong' and 'domain', but that is an error. It is only the habit of using ordinary language that makes those words appear. They are not really there. That is a proposition of pure logic. It does not mention any particular thing at all. This is to be understood as being asserted whatever $x$ and $R$ and $y$ may be. All the statements of logic are of that sort.

It is not a very easy thing to see what are the constituents of a logical proposition. When one takes 'Socrates loves Plato', 'Socrates' is a constituent, 'loves' is a constituent, and 'Plato' is a constituent. Then you turn 'Socrates' into $x$, 'loves' into $R$, and 'Plato' into $y$. $x$ and $R$ and $y$ are nothing, and they are not constituents, so it seems as though all the propositions of logic were entirely devoid of constituents. I do not think that can quite be true. But then the only other thing you can seem to say is that the *form* is a constituent, that propositions of a certain form are always true: that *may* be the right analysis, though I very much doubt whether it is.

There is, however, just this to observe, viz., that the form of a proposition is never a constituent of that proposition itself. If you assert that 'Socrates loves Plato', the form of that proposition is the form of the dual relation, but this is not a constituent of the proposition. If it were you would have to have that constituent related to the other constituents. You will make the form much too substantial if you think of it as really one of the things that have that form, so that the form of a proposition is certainly not a constituent of the proposition itself. Nevertheless it may possibly be a constituent of general statements about propositions that have that form, so I think it is *possible that* logical propositions might be interpreted as being about forms.

I can only say, in conclusion, as regards the constituents of logical propositions, that is a problem which is rather new. There has not been much opportunity to consider it. I do not think any literature exists at all which deals with it in any way whatever, and it is an interesting problem.

I just want now to give you a few illustrations of propositions which can be expressed in the language of pure variables but are not propositions of logic. Among the propositions that are propositions of logic are included all the propositions of pure mathematics, all of which cannot only be expressed in logical terms but can also be deduced from the premisses of logic, and therefore they are logical propositions. Apart from them there are many that can be expressed in logical terms, but cannot be proved from logic, and are certainly not propositions that form part of logic. Suppose you take such proposition as: 'There is at least one thing in the world.' That is a proposition that you can express in logical terms. It will mean, if you like, that the propositional function '$x=x$' is a possible one. That is a proposition, therefore, that you can express in logical terms; but you cannot know from logic whether it is true or false. So far as you do know it, you know it empirically, because there might happen not to be a universe, and then it would not be true. It is merely an accident, so to speak, that there is a universe. The proposition that there are exactly 30,000 things in the world can also be expressed in purely logical terms, and is certainly not a proposition of logic but an empirical proposition (true or false), because a world containing more than 30,000 things and a world containing fewer than 30,000 things are both possible, so that if it happens that there are exactly 30,000 things, that is what one might call an accident and is not a proposition of logic. There are again two propositions that one is used to in mathematical logic, namely, the multiplicative axiom and the axiom of infinity. These also can be expressed in logical terms, but cannot be proved or disproved by logic. In regard to the axiom of infinity, the impossibility of logical proof or disproof may be taken as certain, but in the case of the multiplicative axiom, it is perhaps still open to some degree of doubt. Everything that is a proposition of logic has got to be in some sense or other like a tautology. It has got to be something that has some peculiar quality, which I do not know how to define, that belongs to logical propositions and not to others. Examples of typical logical propositions are:

'If $p$ implies $q$ and $q$ implies $r$, then $p$ implies $r$.'
'If all $a$'s are $b$'s and all $b$'s are $c$'s, then all $a$'s are $c$'s.'
'If all $a$'s are $b$'s and $x$ is an $a$, then $x$ is a $b$.'

Those are propositions of logic. They have a certain peculiar quality which marks them out from other propositions and enables us to know them *a priori*. But what exactly that characteristic is, I am not able to tell you. Although it is a necessary characteristic of logical propositions that they should consist solely of variables, i.e. that they should assert the universal truth, or the sometimes-truth, of a propositional function consisting wholly of variables—although that is a necessary characteristic, it is not a sufficient one. I am sorry that I have had to leave so many problems unsolved. I always have to make this apology, but the world really is rather puzzling and I cannot help it.

### Discussion

*Question:* Is there any word you would substitute for 'existence' which would give existence to individuals? Are you applying the word 'existence' to two ideas, or do you deny that there are two ideas?

*Mr. Russell:* No, there is not an idea that will apply to individuals. As regards the actual things there are in the world, there is nothing at all you can say about them that in any way corresponds to this notion of existence. It is a sheer mistake to say that there is anything analogous to existence that you can say about them. You get into confusion through language, because it is a perfectly correct thing to say 'All the things in the world exist', and it is so easy to pass from this to 'This exists because it is a thing in the world'. There is no sort of point in a predicate which could not conceivably be false. I mean, it is perfectly clear that, if there were such a thing as this existence of individuals that we talk of, it would be absolutely impossible for it not to apply, and that is the characteristic of a mistake.

## VI. Descriptions and Incomplete Symbols

I am proposing to deal this time with the subject of descriptions, and what I call 'incomplete symbols', and the existence of described individuals. You will remember that last time I dealt with the existence of *kinds* of things, what you mean by saying 'There are men' or 'There are Greeks' or phrases of that sort, where you have an existence which may be plural. I am going to deal today with an existence which is asserted to be singular, such as 'The man with the iron mask existed' or some phrase of that sort, where you have some object described by the phrase 'The so-and-so' in the singular, and I want to discuss the analysis of propositions in which phrases of that kind occur.

There are, of course, a great many propositions very familiar in metaphysics which are of that sort: 'I exist' or 'God exists' or 'Homer existed', and other such statements are always occurring in metaphysical discussions, and are, I think, treated in ordinary metaphysics in a way which embodies a simple logical mistake that we shall be concerned with today, the same sort of mistake that I spoke of last week in connection with the existence of kinds of things. One way of examining a proposition of that sort is to ask yourself what would happen if it were false. If you take such a proposition as 'Romulus existed', probably most of us think that Romulus did not exist. It is obviously a perfectly significant statement, whether true or false, to say that Romulus existed. If Romulus himself entered into our statement, it would be plain that the statement that he did not exist would be nonsense, because you cannot have a constituent of a proposition which is nothing at all. Every constituent has got to be there as one of the things in the world, and therefore if Romulus himself entered into the propositions that he existed or that he did not exist, both these propositions could not only not be true, but could not be even significant, unless he existed. That is obviously not the case, and the first conclusion one draws is that, although it *looks* as if Romulus were a constituent of that proposition, that is really a mistake. Romulus does not occur in the proposition 'Romulus did not exist'.

Suppose you try to make out what you do mean by that proposition. You can take, say, all the things that Livy has to say about Romulus, all the properties he ascribes to him, including the only one probably that most of us remember, namely, the fact that he was called 'Romulus'. You can put all this together, and make a propositional function saying '$x$ has such-and-such properties', the properties being those you find enumerated in Livy. There you have a propositional function, and when you say that Romulus did not exist you are simply saying that that propositional function is never true, that it is impossible in the sense I was explaining last time, i.e. that there is no value of $x$ that makes it true. That reduces the non-existence of Romulus to the sort of non-existence I spoke of last time, where we had the non-existence of unicorns. But it is not a *complete* account of this kind of existence or non-existence, because there is one other way in which a described individual can fail to exist, and that is where the description applies to more than one person. You cannot, e.g. speak of '*The* inhabitant of London', not because there are none, but because there are so many.

You see, therefore, that this proposition 'Romulus existed' or 'Romulus did not exist' does introduce a propositional function, because the name 'Romulus' is not really a name but a sort of truncated description. It stands for a person who did such-and-such things, who killed Remus, and founded Rome, and so on. It is short for that description; if you like, it is short for 'the person who was called "Romulus".' If it were really a name, the question of existence could not arise, because a name has got to name something or it is not a name, and if there is no such person as Romulus there cannot be a name for that person who is not there, so that this single word 'Romulus' is really a sort of truncated or telescoped description, and if you think of it as a name you will get into logical errors. When you realize that it is a description, you realize there-

fore that any proposition about Romulus really introduces
the propositional function embodying the description, as
(say) '*x* was called "Romulus"'. That introduces you at
once to a propositional function, and when you say 'Romulus did not exist', you mean that this propositional function
is not true for one value of *x*.

There are two sorts of descriptions, what one may call
'ambiguous descriptions', when we speak of '*a* so-and-so',
and what one may call 'definite descriptions', when we
speak of '*the* so-and-so' (in the singular). Instances are:

*Ambiguous:* A man, a dog, a pig, a Cabinet Minister.

*Definite:*    The man with the iron mask.
           The last person who came into this room.
           The only Englishman who ever occupied
              the Papal See.
           The number of the inhabitants of London.
           The sum of 43 and 34.

(It is not necessary for a description that it should describe
an individual: it may describe a predicate or a relation or
anything else.)

It is phrases of that sort, definite descriptions, that I
want to talk about today. I do not want to talk about
ambiguous descriptions, as what there was to say about
them was said last time.

I want you to realize that the question whether a phrase
is a definite description turns only upon its form, not upon
the question whether there is a definite individual so described. For instance, I should call 'The inhabitant of London' a definite description, although it does not in fact
describe any definite individual.

The first thing to realize about a definite description is
that it is not a name. We will take 'The author of *Waverley*'. That is a definite description, and it is easy to see that
it is not a name. A name is a simple symbol (i.e. a symbol
which does not have any parts that are symbols), a simple
symbol used to designate a certain particular or by exten-

sion an object which is not a particular but is treated for the moment as if it were, or is falsely believed to be a particular, such as a person. This sort of phrase, 'The author of *Waverly*', is not a name because it is a complex symbol. It contains parts which *are* symbols. It contains four words, and the meanings of those four words are already fixed and they have fixed the meaning of 'The author of *Waverley*' in the only sense in which that phrase does have any meaning. In that sense, its meaning is already determinate, i.e. there is nothing arbitrary or conventional about the meaning of that whole phrase, when the meanings of 'the', 'author', 'of', and '*Waverley*' have already been fixed. In that respect, it differs from 'Scott', because when you have fixed the meaning of all the other words in the language, you have done nothing towards fixing the meaning of the name 'Scott'. That is to say, if you understand the English language, you would understand the meaning of the phrase 'The author of *Waverley*' if you had never heard it before, whereas you would not understand the meaning of 'Scott' if you had never heard the word before because to know the meaning of a name is to know who it is applied to.

You sometimes find people speaking as if descriptive phrases were names, and you will find it suggested, e.g. that such a proposition as 'Scott is the author of *Waverley*' really asserts that 'Scott' and the 'the author of *Waverley*' are two names for the same person. That is an entire delusion; first of all, because 'the author of *Waverley*' is not a name, and, secondly, because, as you can perfectly well see, if that were what is meant, the proposition would be one like 'Scott is Sir Walter', and would not depend upon any fact except that the person in question was so called, because a name is what a man is called. As a matter of fact, Scott was the author of *Waverley* at a time when no one called him so, when no one knew whether he was or not, and the fact that he was the author was a physical fact, the fact that he sat down and wrote it with his own hand, which does not have anything to do with what he was called. It is in no way arbitrary. You cannot settle by any choice of nomenclature whether he is or is not to be the author of *Waverley,* because in actual fact he chose to write it and you cannot help yourself. That illustrates how 'the author of *Waverley*' is quite a different thing from a name. You can prove this point very clearly by formal arguments. In 'Scott is the author of *Waverley*' the 'is', of course, expresses identity, i.e. the entity whose name is Scott is identical with the author of *Waverley*. But, when I say 'Scott is mortal' this 'is', is the 'is' of predication, which is quite different from the 'is' of identity. It is a mistake to interpret 'Scott is mortal' as meaning 'Scott is identical with one among mortals', because (among other reasons) you will not be able to say what 'mortals' are except by means of the propositional function '$x$ is mortal', which brings back the 'is' of predication. You cannot reduce the 'is' of predication to the other 'is'. But the 'is' in 'Scott is the author of *Waverley*' is the 'is' of identity and not of predication.[7]

If you were to try to substitute for 'the author of *Waverley*' in that proposition any name whatever, say '$c$', so that the proposition becomes 'Scott is $c$', then if '$c$', is a name for anybody who is not Scott, that proposition would become false, while if, on the other hand, '$c$' is a name for Scott, then the proposition will become simply a tautology. It is at once obvious that if '$c$' were 'Scott' itself, 'Scott is Scott' is just a tautology. But if you take any other name which is just a name for Scott, then if the name is being used *as* a name and not as a description, the proposition will still be a tautology. For the name itself is merely a means of pointing to the thing, and does not occur in what you are asserting, so that if one thing has two names, you make exactly the same assertion whichever of the two names you use, provided they are really names and not truncated descriptions.

_____

[7] The confusion of these two meanings of 'is' is essential to the Hegelian conception of identity-in-difference.

So there are only two alternatives. If 'c' is a name, the proposition 'Scott is c' is either false or tautologous. But the proposition 'Scott is the author of *Waverley*' is neither, and therefore is not the same as any proposition of the form 'Scott is c', where 'c' is a name. That is another way of illustrating the fact that a description is quite a different thing from a name.

I should like to make clear what I was saying just now, that if you substitute another name in place of 'Scott' which is also a name of the same individual, say, 'Scott is Sir Walter', then 'Scott' and 'Sir Walter' are being used as names and not as descriptions, your proposition is strictly a tautology. If one asserts 'Scott is Sir Walter', the way one would mean it would be that one was using the names as descriptions. One would mean that the person called 'Scott' is the person called 'Sir Walter', and 'the person called "Scott" ' is a description, and so is 'the person called "Sir Walter" '. So that would not be a tautology. It would mean that the person called 'Scott' is identical with the person called 'Sir Walter'. But if you are using both as names, the matter is quite different. You must observe that the name does not occur in that which you assert when you use the name. The name is merely that which is a means of expressing what it is you are trying to assert, and when I say 'Scott wrote *Waverley*', the name 'Scott' does not occur in the thing I am asserting. The thing I am asserting is about the person, not about the name. So if I say 'Scott is Sir Walter', using these two names *as* names, neither 'Scott' nor 'Sir Walter' occurs in what I am asserting, but only the person who has these names, and thus what I am asserting is a pure tautology.

It is rather important to realize this about the two different uses of names or of any other symbols: the one when you are talking about the symbol and the other when you are using it *as* a symbol, as a means of talking about something else. Normally, if you talk about your dinner, you are not talking about the word 'dinner' but about what you are going to eat, and that is a different thing altogether. The ordinary use of words is as a means of getting through to things, and when you are using words in that way the statement 'Scott is Sir Walter' is a pure tautology, exactly on the same level as 'Scott is Scott'.

That brings me back to the point that when you take 'Scott is the author of *Waverley*' and you substitute for 'the author of *Waverley*' a name in the place of a description, you get necessarily either a tautology or a falsehood—a tautology if you substitute 'Scott' or some other name for the same person, and a falsehood if you substitute anything else. But the proposition itself is neither a tautology nor a falsehood, and that shows you that the proposition 'Scott is the author of *Waverley*' is a different proposition from any that can be obtained if you substitute a name in the place of 'the author of *Waverley*'. That conclusion is equally true of any other proposition in which the phrase 'the author of *Waverley*' occurs. If you take any proposition in which that phrase occurs and substitute for that phrase a proper name, whether that name be 'Scott' or any other, you will get a different proposition. Generally speaking, if the name that you substitute is 'Scott', your proposition, if it was true before will remain true, and if it was false before will remain false. But it is a *different* proposition. It is not *always* true that it will remain true or false, as may be seen by the example: 'George IV wished to know if Scott was the author of *Waverley*.' It is not true that George IV wished to know if Scott was Scott. So it is even the case that the truth or the falsehood of a proposition is sometimes changed when you substitute a name of an object for a description of the same object. But in any case it is always a different proposition when you substitute a name for a description.

Identity is a rather puzzling thing at first sight. When you say 'Scott is the author of *Waverley*', you are half-tempted to think there are two people, one of whom is Scott and the other the author of *Waverley*, and they happen to be the same. That is obviously absurd, but that is the sort of way one is always tempted to deal with identity.

When I say 'Scott is the author of *Waverley*' and that 'is' expresses identity, the reason that identity can be asserted there truly and without tautology is just the fact that the one is a name and the other a description. Or they might both be descriptions. If I say 'The author of *Waverley* is the author of *Marmion*', that, of course, asserts identity between two descriptions.

Now the next point that I want to make clear is that when a description (when I say 'description' I mean, for the future, a *definite* description) occurs in a proposition, there is no constituent of that proposition corresponding to that description as a whole. In the true analysis of the proposition, the description is broken up and disappears. That is to say, when I say 'Scott is the author of *Waverley*' it is a wrong analysis of that to suppose that you have there three constituents, 'Scott', 'is', and 'the author of *Waverley*'. That, of course, is the sort of way you might think of analysing. You might admit that 'the author of *Waverley*' was complex and could be further cut up, but you might think the proposition could be split into those three bits to begin with. That is an entire mistake. 'The author of *Waverley*' is not a constituent of the proposition at all. There is no constituent really there corresponding to the descriptive phrase. I will try to prove that to you now.

The first and most obvious reason is that you can have significant propositions denying the existence of 'the so-and-so'. 'The unicorn does not exist.' 'The greatest finite number does not exist.' Propositions of that sort are perfectly significant, are perfectly sober, true, decent propositions, and that could not possibly be the case if the unicorn were a constituent of the proposition, because plainly it could not be a constituent as long as there were not any unicorns. Because the constituents of propositions, of course, are the same as the constituents of the corresponding facts, and since it is a fact that the unicorn does not exist, it is perfectly clear that the unicorn is not a constituent of that fact, because if there were any fact of which the unicorn was a constituent, there would be a unicorn, and it would not be true that it did not exist. That applies in this case of descriptions particularly. Now since it is possible for 'the so-and-so' not to exist and yet for propositions in which 'the so-and-so' occurs to be significant and even true, we must try to see what is meant by saying that the so-and-so does exist.

The occurrence of tense in verbs is an exceedingly annoying vulgarity due to our preoccupation with practical affairs. It would be much more agreeable if they had no tense, as I believe is the case in Chinese, but I do not know Chinese. You ought to be able to say 'Socrates exists in the past', 'Socrates exists in the present' or 'Socrates exists in the future', or simply 'Socrates exists', without any implication of tense, but language does not allow that, unfortunately. Nevertheless, I am going to use language in this tenseless way: when I say 'The so-and-so exists', I am not going to mean that it exists in the present or in the past or in the future, but simply that it exists, without implying anything involving tense.

'The author of *Waverley* exists': there are two things required for that. First of all, what is 'the author of *Waverley*'? It is the person who wrote *Waverley*, i.e. we are coming now to this, that you have a propositional function involved, viz., '*x* writes *Waverley*', and the author of *Waverley* is the person who writes *Waverley*, and in order that the person who writes *Waverley* may exist, it is necessary that this propositional function should have two properties:

1. It must be true for *at least* one *x*.
2. It must be true for *at most* one *x*.

If nobody had ever written *Waverley* the author could not exist, and if two people had written it, *the* author could not exist. So that you want these two properties, the one that it is true for at least one *x*, and the other that it is true for at most one *x*, both of which are required for existence.

The property of being true for at least one *x* is the one we dealt with last time: what I expressed by saying that the propositional function is *possible*. Then we come on to the second condition, that it is true for at most one *x,* and that you can express in this way: 'If *x* and *y* wrote *Waverley,* then *x* is identical with *y,* whatever *x* and *y* may be.' That says that at most one wrote it. It does not say that anybody wrote *Waverley* at all, because if nobody had written it, that statement would still be true. It only says that at most one person wrote it.

The first of these conditions for existence fails in the case of the unicorn, and the second in the case of the inhabitant of London.

We put these two conditions together and get a portmanteau expression including the meaning of both. You can reduce them both down to this, that: '("*x* wrote *Waverley*" is equivalent to "*x* is *c*" whatever *x* may be) is possible in respect of *c*.' That is as simple, I think, as you can make the statement.

You see that means to say that there is some entity *c,* we may not know what it is, which is such that when *x* is *c,* it is true that *x* wrote *Waverley,* and when *x* is not *c,* it is not true that *x* wrote *Waverley,* which amounts to saying that *c* is the only person who wrote *Waverley*; and I say there is a value of *c* which makes that true. So that this whole expression, which is a propositional function about *c,* is *possible* in respect of *c* (in the sense explained last time).

That is what I mean when I say that the author of *Waverley* exists. When I say 'the author of *Waverley* exists', I mean that there is an entity *c* such that '*x* wrote *Waverley*' is true when *x* is *c,* and is false when *x* is not *c.* 'The author of *Waverley*' as a constituent has quite disappeared there, so that when I say 'The author of *Waverley* exists' I am not saying anything about the author of *Waverley.* You have instead this elaborate to-do with propositional functions, and 'the author of *Waverley*' has disappeared. That is why it is possible to say significantly 'The author of *Waverley* did not exist'. It would not be possible if 'the author of *Waverley*' were a constituent of propositions in whose verbal expression this descriptive phrase occurs.

The fact that you can discuss the proposition 'God

exists' is a proof that 'God', as used in that proposition, is a description and not a name. If 'God' were a name, no question as to existence could arise.

I have now defined what I mean by saying that a thing described exists. I have still to explain what I mean by saying that a thing described has a certain property. Supposing you want to say 'The author of *Waverley* was human', that will be represented thus: '("*x* wrote *Waverley*" is equivalent to "*x* is *c*" whatever *x* may be, and *c* is human) is possible with respect to *c*'.

You will observe that what we gave before as the meaning of 'The author of *Waverly* exists' is part of this proposition. It is part of any proposition in which 'the author of *Waverley*' has what I call a 'primary occurrence'. When I speak of a 'primary occurrence' I mean that you are not having a proposition about the author of *Waverley* occurring as a part of some larger proposition, such as 'I believe that the author of *Waverley* was human' or 'I believe that the author of *Waverley* exists'. When it is a primary occurrence, i.e. when the proposition concerning it is not just part of a larger proposition, the phrase which we defined as the meaning of 'The author of *Waverley* exists' will be part of that proposition. If I say the author of *Waverley* was human, or a poet, or a Scotsman, or whatever I say about the author of *Waverley* in the way of a primary occurrence, always this statement of his existence is part of the proposition. In that sense all these propositions that I make about the author of *Waverley* imply that the author of *Waverley* exists. So that any statement in which a description has a primary occurrence implies that the object described exists. If I say, 'The present King of France is bald', that implies that the present King of France exists. If I say, 'The present King of France has a fine head of hair', that also implies that the present King of France exists. Therefore unless you understand how a proposition containing a description is to be denied, you will come to the conclusion that it is not true either that the present King of France is bald or that he is not bald, because if you were to enumerate all the things that are bald you would not find him there, and if you were to enumerate all the things that are not bald, you would not find him there either. The only suggestion I have found for dealing with that on conventional lines is to suppose that he wears a wig. You can only avoid the hypothesis that he wears a wig by observing that the denial of the proposition 'The present King of France is bald'' will not be 'The present King of France is not bald', if you mean by that 'There is such a person as the King of France and that person is not bald'. The reason for this is that when you state that the present King of France is bald you say 'There is a $c$ such that $c$ is now King of France and $c$ is bald' and the denial is not 'There is a $c$ such that $c$ is now King of France and $c$ is not bald'. It is more complicated. It is: 'Either there is not a $c$ such that $c$ is now King of France, or, if there is such a $c$, then $c$ is not bald.' Therefore you see that, if you want to deny the proposition 'The present King of France is bald', you can do it by denying that he exists, instead of by denying that he is bald. In order to deny this statement that the present King of France is bald, which is a statement consisting of two parts, you can proceed by denying either part. You can deny the one part, which would lead you to suppose that the present King of France exists but is not bald, or the other part, which will lead you to the denial that the present King of France exists; and either of those two denials will lead you to the falsehood of the proposition 'The present King of France is bald'. When you say 'Scott is human' there is no possibility of a double denial. The only way you can deny 'Scott is human' is by saying 'Scott is not human'. But where a descriptive phrase occurs, you do have the double possibility of denial.

It is of the utmost importance to realize that 'the so-and-so' does not occur in the analysis of propositions in whose verbal expression it occurs, that when I say, 'The author of *Waverley* is human', 'the author of *Waverley*' is not the subject of that proposition, in the sort of way that Scott would be if I said 'Scott is human', using 'Scott' as a name.

I cannot emphasize sufficiently how important this point is, and how much error you get into metaphysics if you do not realize that when I say, 'The author of *Waverley* is human' that is not a proposition of the same form as 'Scott is human'. It does not contain a constituent 'the author of *Waverley*'. The importance of that is very great for many reasons, and one of them is this question of existence. As I pointed out to you last time, there is a vast amount of philosophy that rests upon the notion that existence is, so to speak, a property that you can attribute to things, and that the things that exist have the property of existence and the things that do not exist do not. That is rubbish, whether you take kinds of things, or individual things described. When I say, e.g. 'Homer existed', I am meaning by 'Homer' some description, say 'the author of the Homeric poems', and I am asserting that those poems were written by one man, which is a very doubtful proposition; but if you could get hold of the actual person who did actually write those poems (supposing there was such a person), to say of him that he existed would be uttering nonsense, not a falsehood but nonsense, because it is only of persons described that it can be significantly said that they exist. Last time I pointed out the fallacy in saying 'Men exist, Socrates is a man, therefore Socrates exists'. When I say 'Homer exists, this is Homer, therefore this exists', that is a fallacy of the same sort. It is an entire mistake to argue: 'This is the author of the Homeric poems and the author of the Homeric poems exists, therefore this exists.' It is only where a propositional function comes in that existence may be significantly asserted. You can assert 'The so-and-so exists', meaning that there is just one $c$ which has those properties, but when you get hold of a $c$ that has them, you cannot say of this $c$ that it exists, because that is nonsense: it is not false, but it has no meaning at all.

So the individuals that there are in the world do not exist, or rather it is nonsense to say that they exist and nonsense to say that they do not exist. It is not a thing you can say when you have named them, but only when you have described them. When you say 'Homer exists', you mean 'Homer' is a description which applies to something. A description when it is fully stated is always of the form 'the so-and-so'.

The sort of things that are like these descriptions in that they occur in words in a proposition, but are not in actual fact constituents of the proposition rightly analysed, things of that sort I call 'incomplete symbols'. There are a great many sorts of incomplete symbols in logic, and they are sources of a great deal of confusion and false philosophy, because people get misled by grammar. You think that the proposition 'Scott is mortal' and the proposition 'The author of *Waverley* is mortal' are of the same form. You think that they are both simple propositions attributing a predicate to a subject. That is an entire delusion: one of them is (or rather might be) and one of them is not. These things, like 'the author of *Waverley*', which I call incomplete symbols, are things that have absolutely no meaning whatsoever in isolation but merely acquire a meaning in context. 'Scott' taken as a name has a meaning all by itself. It stands for a certain person, and there it is. But 'the author of *Waverley*' is not a name, and does not all by itself mean anything at all, because when it is rightly used in propositions, those propositions do not contain any constituent corresponding to it.

There are a great many other sorts of incomplete symbols besides descriptions. These are classes, which I shall speak of next time, and relations taken in extension, and so on. Such aggregations of symbols are really the same thing as what I call 'logical fictions', and they embrace practically all the familar objects of daily life: tables, chairs, Piccadilly, Socrates, and so on. Most of them are either classes, or series, or series of classes. In any case they are all incomplete symbols, i.e. they are aggregations that only have a meaning in use and do not have any meaning in themselves.

It is important, if you want to understand the analysis

of the world, or the analysis of facts, or if you want to have any idea what there really is in the world, to realize how much of what there is in phraseology is of the nature of incomplete symbols. You can see that very easily in the case of 'the author of *Waverley*' because 'the author of *Waverley*' does not stand simply for Scott, nor for anything else. If it stood for Scott, 'Scott is the author of *Waverley*' would be the same proposition as 'Scott is Scott', which it is not, since George IV wished to know the truth of the one and did not wish to know the truth of the other. If 'the author of *Waverley*' stood for anything other than Scott, 'Scott is the author of *Waverley*' would be false, which it is not. Hence you have to conclude that 'the author of *Waverley*' does not, in isolation, really stand for anything at all; and that is the characteristic of incomplete symbols.

## VII. The Theory of Types and Symbolism: Classes

Before I begin today the main subject of my lecture, I should like to make a few remarks in explanation and amplification of what I have said about existence in my previous two lectures. This is chiefly on account of a letter I have received from a member of the class, raising many points which, I think, were present in other minds too.

The *first* point I wish to clear up is this: I did not mean to say that when one says a thing exists, one means the same as when one says it is possible. What I meant was, that the fundamental logical idea, the primitive idea, out of which both those are derived is the same. That is not quite the same thing as to say that the statement that a thing exists is the same as the statement that it is possible, which I do not hold. I used the word 'possible' in perhaps a somewhat strange sense, because I wanted some word for a fundamental logical idea for which no word exists in ordinary language, and therefore if one is to try to express in ordinary language the idea in question, one has to take some word and make it convey the sense that I was giving to the word 'possible', which is by no means the only sense that it has but is a sense that was convenient for my purpose. We say of a propositional function that it is possible, where there are cases in which it is true. That is not exactly the same thing as what one ordinarily means, for instance, when one says that it is possible it may rain tomorrow. But what I contend is, that the ordinary uses of the word 'possible' are derived from this notion by a process. E.g. normally when you say of a proposition that it is possible, you mean something like this: first of all it is implied that you do not know whether it is true or false; and I think it is implied, secondly, that it is one of a class of propositions, some of which are known to be true. When I say, e.g. 'It is possible that it may rain tomorrow'— 'It will rain tomorrow' is one of the class of propositions 'It rains at time $t$', where $t$ is different times. We mean partly that we do not know whether it will rain or whether it will not, but also that we do know that that is the sort of proposition that is quite apt to be true, that it is a value of a propositional function of which we know some value to be true. Many of the ordinary uses of 'possible' come under that head, I think you will find. That is to say, that if you say of a proposition that it is possible, what you have is this: 'There is in this proposition some constituent, which, if you turn it into a variable, will give you a propositional function that is sometimes true.' You ought not therefore to say of a proposition simply that it is possible, but rather that it is possible in respect of such-and-such a constituent. That would be a more full expression.

When I say, for instance, that 'Lions exist', I do not mean the same as if I said that lions were possible; because when you say 'Lions exist', that means that the propositional function '$x$ is a lion' is a possible one in the sense that there are lions, while when you say 'Lions are possible' that is a different sort of statement altogether, not meaning that a casual individual animal may be a lion, but rather that a *sort* of animal may be the *sort* that we call 'lions'. If you say 'Unicorns are possible', e.g., you would mean that you do not know any reason why there should not be unicorns, which is quite a different proposition from 'Unicorns exist'. As to what you would mean by saying that unicorns are possible, it would always come down to the same thing as 'It is possible it may rain tomorrow'. You would mean, the proposition 'There are unicorns' is one of a certain set of propositions some of which are known to be true, and that the description of the unicorn does not contain in it anything that *shows* there could not be such beasts.

When I say a propositional function is possible, meaning there are cases in which it is true, I am consciously using the word 'possible' in an unusual sense, because I want a single word for my fundamental idea, and cannot find any word in ordinary language that expresses what I mean.

*Secondly,* it is suggested that when one says a thing exists, it means that it is in time, or in time and space, at any rate in time. That is a very common suggestion, but I do not think that really there is much to be said for that use of words; in the first place, because if that were all you meant, there would be no need for a separate word. In the second place, because after all in the sense, whatever that sense may be, in which the things are said to exist that one ordinarily regards as existing, one may very well wish to discuss the question whether there are things that exist without being in time. Orthodox metaphysics holds that whatever is really real is not in time, that to be in time is to be more or less unreal, and that what really exists is not in time at all. And orthodox theology holds that God is not in time. I see no reason why you should frame your definition of existence in such a way as to preclude that notion of existence. I am inclined to think that there are things that are not in time, and I should be sorry to use the word existence in that sense when you have already the phrase 'being in time' which quite sufficiently expresses what you mean.

Another objection to that definition is that it does not

in the least fit the sort of use of 'existence' which was underlying my discussion, which is the common one in mathematics. When you take existence-theorems, for instance, as when you say 'An even prime exists', you do not mean that the number two is in time but that you can find a number of which you can say 'This is even and prime'. One does ordinarily in mathematics speak of propositions of that sort as existence-theorems, i.e. you establish that there is an object of such-and-such a sort, that object being, of course, in mathematics a logical object, not a particular, not a thing like a lion or a unicorn, but an object like a function or a number, something which plainly does not have the property of being in time at all, and it is that sort of sense of existence-theorems that is relevant in discussing the meaning of existence as I was doing in the last two lectures. I do, of course, hold that that sense of existence can be carried on to cover the more ordinary uses of existence, and does in fact give the key to what is underlying those ordinary uses, as when one says that 'Homer existed' or 'Romulus did not exist', or whatever we may say of that kind.

I come now to a *third* suggestion about existence, which is also a not uncommon one, that of a given particular 'this' you can say 'This exists' in the sense that it is not a phantom or an image or a universal. Now I think that use of existence involves confusions which it is exceedingly important to get out of one's mind, really rather dangerous mistakes. In the first place, we must separate phantoms and images from universals; they are on a different level. Phantoms and images do undoubtedly exist in that sense, whatever it is, in which ordinary objects exist. I mean, if you shut your eyes and imagine some visual scene, the images that are before your mind while you are imagining are undoubtedly there. They are images, something is happening, and what is happening is that the images are before your mind, and these images are just as much part of the world as tables and chairs and anything else. They are perfectly decent objects, and you only call them unreal (if you call them so), or treat them as non-existent, because they do not have the usual sort of relations to other objects. If you shut your eyes and imagine a visual scene and you stretch out your hand to touch what is imaged, you won't get a tactile sensation, or even necessarily a tactile image. You will not get the usual correlation of sight and touch. If you imagine a heavy oak table, you can remove it without any muscular effort, which is not the case with oak tables that you actually see. The general correlations of your images are quite different from the correlations of what one chooses to call 'real' objects. But that is not to say images are unreal. It is only to say they are not part of physics. Of course, I know that this belief in the physical world has established a sort of reign of terror. You have got to treat with disrespect whatever does not fit into the physical world. But that is really very unfair to the things that do not fit in. They are just as much there as the things that do. The physical world is a sort of governing aristocracy, which has somehow managed to cause everything else to be treated with disrespect. That sort of attitude is unworthy of a philosopher. We should treat with exactly equal respect the things that do not fit in with the physical world, and images are among them.

'Phantoms', I suppose, are intended to differ from 'images' by being of the nature of hallucinations, things that are not merely imagined but that go with belief. They again are perfectly real; the only odd thing about them is their correlations. Macbeth sees a dagger. If he tried to touch it, he would not get any tactile sensation, but that does not imply that he was not *seeing* a dagger, it only implies that he was not *touching* it. It does not in any way imply that the visual sensation was not there. It only means to say that the sort of correlation between sight and touch that we are used to is the normal rule but not a universal one. In order to pretend that it is universal, we say that a thing is unreal when it does not fit in. You say, 'Any man who is a man will do such-and-such a thing.' You then find a man who will not, and you say, he is not a man. That is just the same sort of thing as with these daggers that you cannot touch.

I have explained elsewhere the sense in which phantoms are unreal.[8] When you see a 'real' man, the immediate object that you see is one of a whole system of particulars, all of which belong together and make up collectively the various 'appearances' of the man to himself and others. On the other hand, when you see a phantom of a man, that is an isolated particular, not fitting into a system as does a particular which one calls an appearance of the 'real' man. The phantom is in itself just as much part of the world as the normal sense-datum, but it lacks the usual correlation and therefore gives rise to false inferences and becomes deceptive.

As to universals, when I say of a particular that it exists, I certainly do not mean the same thing as if I were to say that it is not a universal. The statement concerning any particular that it is not a universal is quite strictly nonsense—not false, but strictly and exactly nonsense. You never can place a particular in the sort of place where a universal ought to be, and vice versa. If I say 'a is not b', or if I say 'a is b' that implies that a and b are of the same logical type. When I say of a universal that it exists, I should be meaning it in a different sense from that in which one says that particulars exist. E.g. you might say, 'Colours exist in the spectrum between blue and yellow.' That would be a perfectly respectable statement, the colours being taken as universals. You mean simply that the propositional function 'x is a colour between blue and yellow' is one which is capable of truth. But the x which occurs there is not a particular, it is a universal. So that you arrive at the fact that the ultimate important notion involved in existence is the notion that I developed in the lecture before last, the notion of a propositional function being

---

[8]See *Our Knowledge of the External World*, Chap. III. Also Section XII of 'Sense-Data and Physics' in *Mysticism and Logic*.

sometimes true, or being, in other words, possible. The distinction between what some people would call real existence, and existence in people's imagination or in my subjective activity, that distinction, as we have just seen, is entirely one of correlation. I mean that anything which appears to you, you will be mistakenly inclined to say has some more glorified form of existence if it is associated with those other things I was talking of in the way that the appearance of Socrates to you would be associated with his appearance to other people. You would say he was only in your imagination if there were not those other correlated appearances that you would naturally expect. But that does not mean that the appearance to you is not exactly as much a part of the world as if there were other correlated appearances. It will be exactly as much a part of the real world, only it will fail to have the correlations that you expect. That applies to the question of sensation and imagination. Things imagined do not have the same sort of correlations as things sensated. If you care to see more about this question, I wrote a discussion in *The Monist* for January 1915, and if any of you are interested, you will find the discussion there.

I come now to the proper subject of my lecture, but shall have to deal with it rather hastily. It was to explain the theory of types and the definition of classes. Now first of all, as I suppose most of you are aware, if you proceed carelessly with formal logic, you can very easily get into contradictions. Many of them have been known for a long time, some even since the time of the Greeks, but it is only fairly recently that it has been discovered that they bear upon mathematics, and that the ordinary mathematician is liable to fall into them when he approaches the realms of logic, unless he is very cautious. Unfortunately the mathematical ones are more difficult to expound, and the ones easy to expound strike one as mere puzzles or tricks.

You can start with the question whether or not there is a greatest cardinal number. Every class of things that you can choose to mention has some cardinal number. That follows very easily from the definition of cardinal numbers as classes of similar classes, and you would be inclined to suppose that the class of all the things there are in the world would have about as many members as a class could be reasonably expected to have. The plain man would suppose you could not get a larger class than the class of all the things there are in the world. On the other hand, it is very easy to prove that if you take selections of some of the members of a class, making those selections in every conceivable way that you can, the number of different selections that you can make is greater than the original numbers of terms. That is easy to see with small numbers. Suppose you have a class with just three members, $a, b, c$. The first selection that you can make is the selection of no terms. The next of $a$ alone, $b$ alone, $c$ alone. Then $bc, ca, ab, abc,$ which makes in all 8 (i.e. $2^3$) selections. Generally speaking, if you have $n$ terms, you can make $2^n$ selections. It is very easy to prove that $2^n$ is always greater than $n$, whether $n$ happens to be finite or not. So you find that the total number of things in the world is not so great as the number of classes that can be made up out of those things. I am asking you to take all these propositions for granted, because there is not time to go into the proofs, but they are all in Cantor's work. Therefore you will find that the total number of things in the world is by no means the greatest number. On the contrary, there is a hierarchy of numbers greater than that. That, on the face of it, seems to land you in a contradiction. You have, in fact, a perfectly precise arithmetical proof that there are *fewer* things in heaven or earth than are dreamt of in *our* philosophy. That shows how philosophy advances.

You are met with the necessity, therefore, of distin-guishing between classes and particulars. You are met with the necessity of saying that a class consisting of two partic-ulars is not itself in turn a fresh particular, and that has to be expanded in all sort of ways; i.e. you will have to say that in the sense in which there are particulars, in that sense it is not true to say there are classes. The sense in

which there are classes is a different one from the sense in
which there are particulars, because if the senses of the two
were exactly the same, a world in which there are three
particulars and therefore eight classes, would be a world
in which there are at least eleven things. As the Chinese
philosopher pointed out long ago, a dun cow and a bay
horse make three things: separately they are each one, and
taken together they are another, and therefore three.

I pass now to the contradiction about classes that are
not members of themselves. You would say generally that
you would not expect a class to be a member of itself. For
instance, if you take the class of all the teaspoons in the
world, that is not in itself a teaspoon. Or if you take all the
human beings in the world, the whole class of them is not
in turn a human being. Normally you would say you cannot expect a whole class of things to be itself a member of
that class. But there are apparent exceptions. If you take,
e.g. all the things in the world that are not teaspoons and
make up a class of them, that class obviously (you would
say) will not be a teaspoon. And so generally with negative
classes. And not only with negative classes, either, for if
you think for a moment that classes are things in the same
sense in which things are things, you will then have to say
that the class consisting of all the things in the world is itself
a thing in the world, and that therefore this class is a
member of itself. Certainly you would have thought that
it was clear that the class consisting of all the classes in the
world is itself a class. That I think most people would feel
inclined to suppose, and therefore you would get there a
case of a class which is a member of itself. If there is any
sense in asking whether a class is a member of itself or not,
then certainly in all the cases of the ordinary classes of
everyday life you find that a class is not a member of itself.
Accordingly, that being so, you could go on to make up
the class of all those classes that are not members of themselves, and you can ask yourself, when you have done that,
is that class a member of itself or is it not?

Let us first suppose that it is a member of itself. In that

case it is one of those classes that are not members of themselves, i.e. it is not a member of itself. Let us then suppose that it is not a member of itself. In that case it is not one of those classes that are not members of themselves, i.e. it is one of those classes that are members of themselves, i.e. it is a member of itself. Hence either hypothesis, that it is or that it is not a member of itself, leads to its contradiction. If it is a member of itself, it is not, and if it is not, it is.

That contradiction is extremely interesting. You can modify its form; some forms of modification are valid and some are not. I once had a form suggested to me which was not valid, namely the question whether the barber shaves himself or not. You can define the barber as 'one who shaves all those, and those only, who do not shave themselves'. The question is, does the barber shave himself? In this form the contradiction is not very difficult to solve. But in our previous form I think it is clear that you can only get around it by observing that the whole question whether a class is or is not a member of itself is nonsense, i.e. that no class either is or is not a member of itself, and that it is not even true to say that, because the whole form of words is just a noise without meaning. That has to do with the fact that classes, as I shall be coming on to show, are incomplete symbols in the same sense in which the descriptions are that I was talking of last time; you are talking nonsense when you ask yourself whether a class is or is not a member of itself, because in any full statement of what is meant by a proposition which seems to be about a class, you will find that the class is not mentioned at all and that there is nothing about a class in that statement. It is absolutely necessary, if a statement about a class is to be significant and not pure nonsense, that it should be capable of being translated into a form in which it does not mention the class at all. This sort of statement, 'Such-and-such a class is or is not a member of itself', will not be capable of that kind of translation. It is analogous to what I was saying about descriptions: the symbol for a class is an incomplete symbol; it does not really stand for part of the propositions in which symbolically it occurs, but in the right analysis of those propositions that symbol has been broken up and disappeared.

There is one other of these contradictions that I may as well mention, the most ancient, the saying of Epimenides that 'All Cretans are liars'. Epimenides was a man who slept for sixty years without stopping, and I believe that it was at the end of that nap that he made the remark that all Cretans were liars. It can be put more simply in the form: if a man makes the statement 'I am lying', is he lying or not? If he is, that is what he said he was doing, so he is speaking the truth and not lying. If, on the other hand, he is not lying, then plainly he is speaking the truth in saying that he is lying, and therefore he is lying, since he says truly that that is what he is doing. It is an ancient puzzle, and nobody treated that sort of thing as anything but a joke until it was found that it had to do with such important and practical problems as whether there is a greatest cardinal or ordinal number. Then at last these contradictions were treated seriously. The man who says 'I am lying' is really asserting 'There is a proposition which I am asserting and which is false.' That is presumably what you mean by lying. In order to get out the contradiction you have to take that whole assertion of his as one of the propositions to which his assertion applies; i.e. when he says 'There is a proposition which I am asserting and which is false', the word 'proposition' has to be interpreted as to include among propositions his statement to the effect that he is asserting a false proposition. Therefore you have to suppose that you have a certain totality, viz., that of propositions, but that that totality contains members which can only be defined in terms of itself. Because when you say 'There is a proposition which I am asserting and which is false', that is a statement whose meaning can only be got by reference to the totality of propositions. You are not saying which among all the propositions there are in the world it is that you are asserting and that is false.

Therefore it presupposes that the totality of proposition is spread out before you and that some one, though you do not say which, is being asserted falsely. It is quite clear that you get a vicious circle if you first suppose that this totality of propositions is spread out before you, so that you can without picking any definite one say 'Some one out of this totality is being asserted falsely', and that yet, when you have gone on to say 'Some one out of this totality is being asserted falsely', that assertion is itself one of the totality you were to pick out from. That is exactly the situation you have in the paradox of the liar. You are supposed to be given first of all a set of propositions, and you assert that some one of these is being asserted falsely, then that asser-tion itself turns out to be one of the set, so that it is obviously fallacious to suppose the set already there in its entirety. If you are going to say anything about 'all propo-sitions', you will have to define propositions, first of all, in some such way as to exclude those that refer to all the propositions of the sort already defined. It follows that the word 'proposition', in the sense in which we ordinarily try to use it, is a meaningless one, and that we have got to divide propositions up into sets and can make statements about all propositions in a given set, but those propositions will not themselves be members of the set. For instance, I may say 'All atomic propositions are either true or false', but that itself will not be an atomic proposition. If you try to say 'All propositions are either true or false', without qualification, you are uttering nonsense, because if it were not nonsense it would have to be itself a proposition and one of those included in its own scope, and therefore the law of excluded middle as enunciated just now is a mean-ingless noise. You have to cut propositions up into different types, and you can start with atomic propositions or, if you like, you can start with those propositions that do not refer to sets of propositions at all. Then you will take next those that refer to sets of propositions of that sort that you had first. Those that refer to sets of propositions of the first type, you may call the second type, and so on.

If you apply that to the person who says 'I am lying', you will find that the contradiction has disappeared, because he will have to say what type of liar he is. If he says 'I am asserting a false proposition of the first type', as a matter of fact that statement, since it refers to the totality of propositions of the first type, is of the second type. Hence it is not true that he is asserting a false proposition of the first type, and he remains a liar. Similarly, if he said he was asserting a false proposition of the 30,000th type, that would be a statement of the 30,001st type, so he would still be a liar. And the counter-argument to prove that he was also not a liar has collapsed.

You can lay it down that a totality of any sort cannot be a member of itself. That applies to what we are saying about classes. For instance, the totality of classes in the world cannot be a class in the same sense in which they are. So we shall have to distinguish a hierarchy of classes. We will start with the classes that are composed entirely of particulars: that will be the first type of classes. Then we will go on to classes whose members are classes of the first type: that will be the second type. Then we will go on to classes whose members are classes of the second type: that will be the third type, and so on. Never is it possible for a class of one type either to be or not to be identical with a class of another type. That applies to the question I was discussing a moment ago, as to how many things there are in the world. Supposing there are three particulars in the world. There are then, as I was explaining, 8 classes of particulars. There will be $2^8$ (i.e. 256) classes of classes of particulars, and $2^{256}$ classes of classes of classes of particulars, and so on. You do not get any contradiction arising out of that, and when you ask yourself the question: 'Is there, or is there not a greatest cardinal number?' the answer depends entirely upon whether you are confining yourself within some one type, or whether you are not. Within any given type there is a greater cardinal number, namely, the number of objects of that type, but you will always be able to get a larger number by going up to the next type. Therefore, there is no number so great but what you can get a greater number in a sufficiently high type. There you have the two sides of the argument: the one side when the type is given, the other side when the type is not given.

I have been talking, for brevity's sake, as if there really were all these different sorts of things. Of course, that is nonsense. There are particulars, but when one comes on to classes, and classes of classes, and classes of classes of classes, one is talking of logical fictions. When I say there are no such things, that again is not correct. It is not significant to say 'There are such things', in the same sense of the words 'there are' in which you can say 'There are particulars'. If I say 'There are particulars' and 'There are classes', the two phrases 'there are' will have to have different meanings in those two propositions, and if they have suitable different meanings, both propositions may be true. If, on the other hand, the words 'there are' are used in the same sense in both, then one at least of those statements must be nonsense, not false but nonsense. The question then arises, what is the sense in which one can say 'There are classes', or in other words, what do you mean by a statement in which a class appears to come in? First of all, what are the sort of things you would like to say about classes? They are just the same as the sort of things you want to say about propositional functions. You want to say of a propositional function that it is sometimes true. That is the same thing as saying of a class that it has members. You want to say that is it true for exactly 100 values of the variables. That is the same as saying of a class that it has a hundred members. All the things you want to say about classes are the same as the things you want to say about propositional functions excepting for accidental and irrelevant linguistic forms, with, however, a certain proviso which must now be explained.

Take, e.g. two propositional functions such as '$x$ is a man', '$x$ is a featherless biped'. Those two are formally equivalent, i.e. when one is true so is the other, and vice

versa. Some of the things that you can say about a propsi-
tional function will not necessarily remain true if you
substitute another formally equivalent propositional function in its place. For instance, the propositional function
'x is a man' is one which has to do with the concept of
humanity. That will not be true of 'x is a featherless biped'.
Or if you say, 'so-and-so asserts that such-and-such is a
man' the propositional function 'x is a man' comes in
there, but 'x is a featherless biped' does not. There are a
certain number of things which you can say about a propositional function which would be not true if you substitute
another formally equivalent propositional function. On the
other hand, any statement about a propositional function
which will remain true or remain false, as the case may be,
when you substitute for it another formally equivalent
propositional function, may be regarded as being about
the class which is associated with the propositional function. I want you to take the words *may be regarded* strictly.
I am using them instead of *is,* because *is* would be untrue.
'Extensional' statements about functions are those that
remain true when you substitute any other formally equivalent function, and these are the ones that may be regarded as being about the class. If you have any statement
about a function which is not extensional, you can always
derive from it a somewhat similar statement which is extensional, viz., there is a function formally equivalent to the
one in question about which the statement in question is
true. This statement, which is manufactured out of the one
you started with, will be extensional. It will always be
equally true or equally false of any two formally equivalent
functions, and this derived extensional statement may be
regarded as being the corresponding statement about the
associated class. So, when I say that 'The class of men has
so-and-so many members', that is to say 'There are so-and-
so many men in the world', that will be derived from the
statement that 'x is human' is satisfied by so-and-so many
values of x, and in order to get it into the extensional form,
one will put it in this way, that 'There is a function formally

equivalent to "$x$ is human", which is true for so-and-so many values of $x$.' That I should define as what I mean by saying 'The class of men has so-and-so many members.' In that way you find that all the formal properties that you desire of classes, all their formal uses in mathematics, can be obtained without supposing for a moment that there are such things as classes, without supposing, that is to say, that a proposition in which symbolically a class occurs, does in fact contain a constituent corresponding to that symbol, and when rightly analysed that symbol will disappear, in the same sort of way as descriptions disappear when the propositions are rightly analysed in which they occur.

There are certain difficulties in the more usual view of classes, in addition to those we have already mentioned, that are solved by our theory. One of these concerns the null-class, i.e. the class consisting of no members, which is difficult to deal with on a purely extensional basis. Another is concerned with unit-classes. With the ordinary view of classes you would say that a class that has only one member was the same as that one member. That will land you in terrible difficulties, because in that case that one member is a member of that class, namely, itself. Take, e.g. the class of 'Lecture audiences in Gordon Square'. That is obviously a class of classes, and probably it is a class that has only one member, and that one member itself (so far) has more than one member. Therefore if you were to identify the class of lecture audiences in Gordon Square with the only lecture audience that there is in Gordon Square, you would have to say both that it has one member and that it has twenty members, and you will be landed in contradictions, because this audience has more than one member, but the class of audiences in Gordon Square has only one member. Generally speaking, if you have any collection of many objects forming a class, you can make a class of which that class is the only member, and the class of which that class is the only member will have only one member, though this only member will have many members. This is one reason why you must distinguish a unit-class from its only member. Another is that, if you do not, you will find that the class is a member of itself, which is objectionable, as we saw earlier in this lecture. I have omitted a subtlety connected with the fact that two formally equivalent functions may be of different types. For the way of treating this point, see *Principia Mathematica,* page 20, and Introduction, Chapter III.

I have not said quite all that I ought to have said on this subject. I meant to have gone a little more into the theory of types. The theory of types is really a theory of symbols, not of things. In a proper logical language it would be perfectly obvious. The trouble that there is arises from our inveterate habit of trying to name what cannot be named. If we had a proper logical language, we should not be tempted to do that. Strictly speaking, only particulars can be named. In that sense in which there are particulars, you cannot say either truly or falsely that there is anything else. The word 'there is' is a word having 'systematic ambiguity', i.e. having a strictly infinite number of different meanings which it is important to distinguish.

### Discussion

*Question:* Could you lump all those classes, and classes of classes, and so on, together?

*Mr. Russell:* All are fictions, but they are different fictions in each case. When you say 'There are classes of particulars', the statement 'there are' wants expanding and explaining away, and when you have put down what you really do mean, or ought to mean, you will find that it is something quite different from what you thought. That process of expanding and writing down fully what you mean, will be different if you go on to 'there are classes of classes of particulars'. There are infinite numbers of meanings to 'there are'. The first only is fundamental, so far as the hierarchy of classes is concerned.

*Question:* I was wondering whether it was rather analogous to spaces, where the first three dimensions are actual, and the higher ones are merely symbolic. I see there is a difference, there are higher dimensions, but you can lump those together.

*Mr. Russell:* There is only one fundamental one, which is the first one, the one about particulars, but when you have gone to classes, you have travelled already just as much away from what there is as if you have gone to classes of classes. There are no classes really in the physical world. The particulars are there, but not classes. If you say 'There is a universe' that meaning of 'there is' will be quite different from the meaning in which you say 'There is a particular', which means that 'the propositional function "$x$ is a particular" is sometimes true'.

All those statements are about symbols. They are never about the things themselves, and they have to do with 'types'. This is really important and I ought not to have forgotten to say it, that the relation of the symbol to what it means is different in different types. I am not now talking about this hierarchy of classes and so on, but the relation of a predicate to what it means is different from the relation of a name to what it means. There is not one single concept of 'meaning' as one ordinarily thinks there is, so that you can say in a uniform sense 'All symbols have meaning', but there are infinite numbers of different ways of meaning, i.e. different sorts of relation of the symbol to the symbolized, which are absolutely distinct. The relation, e.g. of a proposition to a fact, is quite different from the relation of a name to a particular, as you can see from the fact that there are two propositions always related to one given fact, and that is not so with names. That shows you that the relation that the proposition has to the fact is quite different from the relation of a name to a particular. You must not suppose that there is, over and above that, another way in which you could get at facts by naming them. You can always only get at the thing you are aiming at by the proper sort of symbol, which approaches it in the appropriate way. That is the real philosophical truth that is at the bottom of all this theory of types.

## VIII. Excursus into Metaphysics: What There Is

I come now to the last lecture of this course, and I propose briefly to point to a few of the morals that are to be gathered from what has gone before, in the way of suggesting the bearing of the doctrines that I have been advocating upon various problems of metaphysics. I have dwelt hitherto upon what one may call philosophical grammar, and I am afraid I have had to take you through a good many very dry and dusty regions in the course of that investigation, but I think the importance of philosophical grammar is very much greater than it is generally thought to be. I think that practically all traditional metaphysics is filled with mistakes due to bad grammar, and that almost all the traditional problems of metaphysics and traditional results—supposed results—of metaphysics are due to a failure to make the kind of distinctions in what we may call philosophical grammar with which we have been concerned in these previous lectures.

Take, as a very simple example, the philosophy of arithmetic. If you think that 1, 2, 3, and 4, and the rest of the numbers, are in any sense entities, if you think that there are objects, having those names, in the realm of being, you have at once a very considerable apparatus for your metaphysics to deal with, and you have offered to you a certain kind of analysis of arithmetical propositions. When you say, e.g. that 2 and 2 are 4, you suppose in that case that you are making a proposition of which the number 2 and the number 4 are constituents, and that has all sorts of consequences, all sorts of bearings upon your general metaphysical outlook. If there has been any truth in the doctrines that we have been considering, all numbers are what I call logical fictions. Numbers are classes of classes, and classes are logical fictions, so that numbers are, as it were, fictions at two removes, fictions of fictions. Therefore you do not have, as part of the ultimate constituents of your world, these queer entities that you are inclined to call numbers. The same applies in many other directions.

One purpose that has run through all that I have said, has been the justification of analysis, i.e. the justification of logical atomism, of the view that you can get down in theory, if not in practice, to ultimate simples, out of which the world is built, and that those simples have a kind of reality not belonging to anything else. Simples, as I tried to explain, are of an infinite number of sorts. There are particulars and qualities and relations of various orders, a whole hierarchy of different sorts of simples, but all of them, if we were right, have in their various ways some kind of reality that does not belong to anything else. The only other sort of object you come across in the world is what we call *facts,* and facts are the sort of things that are asserted or denied by propositions, and are not properly entities at all in the same sense in which their constituents are. That is shown in the fact that you cannot name them. You can only deny, or assert, or consider them, but you cannot name them because they are not there to be named, although in another sense it is true that you cannot know the world unless you know the facts that make up the truths of the world; but the knowing of facts is a different sort of thing from the knowing of simples.

Another purpose which runs through all that I have been saying is the purpose embodied in the maxim called Occam's Razor. That maxim comes in, in practice, in this way: take some science, say physics. You have there a given body of doctrine, a set of propositions expressed in symbols—I am including words among symbols—and you think that you have reason to believe that on the whole those propositions, rightly interpreted, are fairly true, but you do not know what is the actual meaning of the symbols that you are using. The meaning they have *in use* would have to be explained in some pragmatic way: they have a certain kind of practical or emotional significance to you which is a datum, but the logical significance is not a datum, but a thing to be sought, and you go through, if you are analysing a science like physics, these propositions with a view to finding out what is the smallest empirical apparatus—or the smallest apparatus, not necessarily wholly empirical—out of which you can build up these propositions. What is the smallest number of simple undefined things at the start, and the smallest number of undemonstrated premisses, out of which you can define the things that need to be defined and prove the things that need to be proved? That problem, in any case that you like to take, is by no means a simple one, but on the contrary an extremely difficult one. It is one which requires a very great amount of logical technique; and the sort of thing that I have been talking about in these lectures is the preliminaries and first steps in that logical technique. You cannot possibly get at the solution of such a problem as I am talking about if you go at it in a straightforward fashion with just the ordinary acumen that one accumulates in the course of reading or in the study of traditional philosophy. You do need this apparatus of symbolical logic that I have been talking about. (The description of the subject as symbolical logic is an inadequate one. I should like to describe it simply as logic, on the ground that nothing else really is logic, but that would sound so arrogant that I hesitate to do so.)

Let us consider further the example of physics for a moment. You find, if you read the words of physicists, that they reduce matter down to certain elements—atoms, ions, corpuscles, or what not. But in any case the sort of thing that you are aiming at in the physical analysis of matter is to get down to very little bits of matter that still are just like matter in the fact that they persist through time, and that they travel about in space. They have in fact all the ordinary everyday properties of physical matter, not the matter that one has in ordinary life—they do not taste or smell or appear to the naked eye—but they have the properties that you very soon get to when you travel towards physics from ordinary life. Things of that sort, I say, are not the ultimate constituents of matter in any metaphysical sense. Those things are all of them, as I think a very little reflection shows, logical fictions in the sense that I was speaking of. At least, when I say they are, I speak somewhat too dogmatically. It is possible that there may be all these things that the physicist talks about in actual reality, but it is impossible that we should ever have any reason whatsoever for supposing that there are. That is the situation that you arrive at generally in such analyses. You find that a certain thing which has been set up as a metaphysical entity can either be assumed dogmatically to be real, and then you will have no possible argument either for its reality or against its reality; or, instead of doing that, you can construct a logical fiction having the same formal properties, or rather having formally analogous formal properties to those of the supposed metaphysical entity and itself composed of empirically given things, and that logical fiction can be substituted for your supposed metaphysical entity and will fulfil all the scientific purposes that anybody can desire. With atoms and the rest it is so, with all the metaphysical entities whether of science or of metaphysics. By metaphysical entities I mean those things which are supposed to be part of the ultimate constituents of the world, but not to be the kind of thing that is ever empirically given—I do not say merely not being itself empirically given, but not being the *kind* of thing that is empirically given. In the case of matter, you can start from what is empirically given, what one sees and hears and smells and so forth, all the ordinary data of sense, or you can start with some definite ordinary object, say this desk, and you can ask yourselves, 'What do I mean by saying that this desk that I am looking at now is the same as the one I was looking at a week ago?' The first simple ordinary answer would be that it *is* the same desk, it is actually identical, there is a perfect identity of substance, or whatever you like to call it. But when that apparently simple answer is suggested, it is important to observe that you cannot have an empirical reason for such a view as that, and if you hold it, you hold it simply because you like it and for no other reason whatever. All that you really know is such facts as that what you see now, when you look at the desk, bears a very close similarity to what you saw a week ago when you looked at it. Rather more than that one fact of similarity I admit you know, or you may know. You might have paid some one to watch the desk continuously throughout the week, and might then have discovered that it was presenting appearances of the same sort all through that period, assuming that the light was kept on all through the night. In that way you could have established continuity. You have not in fact done so. You do not in fact know that that desk has gone on looking the same all the time, but we will assume that. Now the essential point is this: What is the empirical reason that makes you call a number of appearances, appearances of the same desk? What makes you say on successive occasions, I am seeing the same desk? The first thing to notice is this, that it does not matter what is the answer, so long as you have realized that the answer consists in something empirical and not in a recognized metaphysical identity of substance. There is something given in experience which makes you call it the same desk, and having once grasped that fact, you can go on and say, it is that something (whatever it is) that makes you call it the same desk which shall be *defined* as *constituting* it the same desk, and there shall be no assumption of a metaphysical substance which is identical throughout. It is a little easier to the untrained mind to conceive of an identity than it is to conceive of a system of correlated particulars, hung one to another by relations of similarity and continuous change and so on. That idea is apparently more complicated, but that is what is empirically given in the real world, and substance, in the sense of something which is continuously identical in the same desk, is not given to you. Therefore in all cases where you seem to have a continuous entity persisting through changes, what you have to do is to ask yourself what makes you consider the successive appearances as belonging to one thing. When you have found out what makes you take the view that they belong to the same thing, you will then see that that which has made you say so, is all that is *certainly* there in the way of unity. Anything that there may be over and above that, I shall recognize as something I cannot know. What I can know is that there are a certain series of appearances linked together, and the series of those appearances I shall define as being a desk. In that way the desk is reduced to being a logical fiction, because a series is a logical fiction. In that way all the ordinary objects of daily life are extruded from the world of what there is, and in their place as what there is you find a number of passing particulars of the kind that one is immediately conscious of in sense. I want to make clear that I am not *denying* the existence of anything; I am only refusing to affirm it. I refuse to affirm the existence of anything for which there is no evidence, but I equally refuse to deny the existence of anything against which there is no evidence. Therefore I neither affirm nor deny it, but merely say, that is not in the realm of the knowable and is certainly not a part of physics; and physics, if it is to be interpreted, must be interpreted in terms of the sort of thing that can be empirical. If your atom is going to serve purposes in physics, as it undoubtedly does, your atom has got to turn out to be a construction, and your atom will in fact turn out to be a series of classes of particulars. The same process which one applies to physics, one will also apply elsewhere. The application to physics I explained briefly in my book on the *External World,* Chapters III and IV.

I have talked so far about the unreality of the things we think real. I want to speak with equal emphasis about the reality of things we think unreal such as phantoms and hallucinations. Phantoms and hallucinations, considered in themselves, are, as I explained in the preceding lectures, on exactly the same level as ordinary sense-data. They differ from ordinary sense-data only in the fact that they do not have the usual correlations with other things. In themselves they have the same reality as ordinary sense-data. They have the most complete and absolute and perfect reality that anything can have. They are part of the ultimate constituents of the world, just as the fleeting sense-data are. Speaking of the fleeting sense-data, I think it is very important to remove out of one's instincts any disposition to believe that the real is the permanent. There had been a metaphysical prejudice always that if a thing is really real, it has to last either forever or for a fairly decent length of time. That is to my mind an entire mistake. The things that are really real last a very short time. Again I am not denying that there *may* be things that last forever, or for thousands of years; I only say that those are not within our experience, and that the real things that we know by experience last for a very short time, one tenth or half a second, or whatever it may be. Phantoms and hallucinations are among those, among the ultimate constituents of the world. The things that we call real, like tables and chairs, are systems, series of classes of particulars, and the particulars are the real things, the particulars being sense-data when they happen to be given to you. A table or chair will be a series of classes of particulars, and therefore a logical fiction. Those particulars will be on the same level of reality as a hallucination or a phantom. I ought to explain in what sense a chair is a series of classes. A chair presents at each moment a number of different appearances. All the appearances that it is presenting at a given moment make up a certain class. All those sets of appearances vary from time to time. If I take a chair and smash it, it will present a whole set of different appearances from what it did before, and without going as far as that, it will always be changing as the light changes, and so on. So you get a series in time of different sets of appearances, and that is what I mean by saying that a chair is a series of classes. That explanation is too crude, but I leave out the niceties, as that is not the actual topic I am dealing with. Now each single particular which is part of this whole system is linked up with the others in the system. Supposing, e.g. I take as my particular the appearance which that chair is presenting to me at this moment. That is linked up first of all with the appearance which the same chair is presenting to any one of you at the same moment, and with the appearance which it is going to present to me at later moments. There you get at once two journeys that you can take away from that particular, and that particular will be correlated in certain definite ways with the other particulars which also belong to that chair. That is what you mean by saying—or what you ought to mean by saying—that what I see before me is a real thing as opposed to a phantom. It means that it has a whole set of correlations of different kinds. It means that that particular, which is the appearance of the chair to me at this moment, is not isolated but is connected in a certain well-known familiar fashion with others, in the sort of way that makes it answer one's expectations. And so, when you go and buy a chair, you buy not only the appearance which it presents to you at that moment, but also those other appearances that it is going to present when it gets home. If it were a phantom chair, it would not present any appearances when it got home, and would not be the sort of thing you would want to buy. The sort one calls real is one of a whole correlated system, whereas the sort you call hallucinations are not. The respectable particulars in the world are all of them linked up with other particulars in respectable, conventional ways. Then sometimes you get a wild particular, like a merely visual chair that you cannot sit on, and say it is a phantom, a hallucination, you exhaust all the vocabulary of abuse upon it. That is what one means by calling it unreal, because 'unreal' applied in that way is a term of abuse and never would be applied to a thing that *was* unreal because you would not be so angry with it.

I will pass on to some other illustrations. Take a person. What is it that makes you say when you meet your friend Jones, 'Why, this is Jones'? It is clearly not the persistence of a metaphysical entity inside Jones somewhere, because even if there be such an entity, it certainly is not what you see when you see Jones coming along the street; it certainly is something that you are not acquainted with, not an empirical datum. Therefore plainly there is something in the empirical appearances which he presents to you, something in their relations one to another, which enables you to collect all these together and say, 'These are what I call the appearances of one person', and that something that makes you collect them together is not the persistence of a metaphysical subject, because that, whether there be such a persistent subject or not, is certainly not a datum, and that which makes you say 'Why, it is Jones' is a datum. Therefore Jones is not constituted as he is known by a sort of pin-point ego that is underlying his appearances, and you have got to find some correlations among the appearances which are of the sort that make you put all those appearances together and say, they are the appearances of one person. Those are different when it is other people and when it is yourself. When it is yourself, you have more to go by. You have not only what you look like, you have also your thoughts and memories and all your organic sensations, so that you have a much richer material and are therefore much less likely to be mistaken as to your own identity than as to someone else's. It happens, of course, that there are mistakes even as to one's own identity, in cases of multiple personality and so forth, but as a rule you will know that it is you because you have more to go by than other people have, and you would know it is you, not by a consciousness of the ego at all but by all sorts of things, by memory, by the way you feel and the way you look and a host of things. But all those are empirical data, and those enable you to say that the person to whom something happened yesterday was yourself. So you can collect a whole set of experiences into one string as all belonging to you, and similarly other people's experiences can be collected together as all belonging to them by relations that actually are observable and without assuming the existence of the persistent ego. It does not matter in the least to what we are concerned with, what exactly is the given empirical relation between two experiences that make us say, 'These are two experiences of the same person.' It does not matter precisely what that relation is, because the logical formula for the construction of the person is the same whatever that relation may be, and because the mere fact that you can know that two experiences belong to the same person proves that there is such an empirical relation to be ascertained by analysis. Let us call the relation *R*. We shall say that when two experiences have to each other the relation *R*, then they are said to be experiences of the same person. That is a definition of what I mean by 'experiences of the same person'. We proceed here just in the same way as when we are defining numbers. We first define what is meant by saying that two classes 'have the same number', and then define what a number is. The person who has a given experience *x* will be the class of all those experiences which are 'experiences of the same person' as the one who experiences *x*. You can say that two events are co-personal when there is between them a certain relation *R*, namely that relation which makes us say that they are experiences of the same person. You can define the person who has a certain experience as being those experiences that are co-personal with that experience, and it will be better perhaps to take them as a series than as a class, because you want to know which is the beginning of a man's life and which is the end. Therefore we shall say that a person is a certain series of experiences. We shall not deny that there may be a metaphysical ego. We shall merely say that it is a question that does not concern us in any way, because it is a matter about which we know nothing and can know nothing, and therefore it obviously cannot be a thing that comes into science in any way. What we know is this string of experiences that makes up a person, and that is put together by means of certain empirically given relations such, e.g. as memory.

I will take another illustration, a kind of problem that our method is useful in helping to deal with. You all know the American theory of neutral monism, which derives really from William James and is also suggested in the work of Mach, but in a rather less developed form. The theory of neutral monism maintains that the distinction between the mental and the physical is entirely an affair of arrangement, that the actual material arranged is exactly the same in the case of the mental as it is in the case of the physical, but they differ merely in the fact that when you take a thing as belonging in the same context with certain other things, it will belong to psychology, while when you take it in a certain other context with other things, it will belong to physics, and the difference is as to what you consider to be its context, just the same sort of difference as there is between arranging the people in London alphabetically or geographically. So, according to William James, the actual material of the world can be arranged in two different ways, one of which gives you physics and the other psychology. It is just like rows or columns: in an arrangement of rows and columns, you can take an item as either a member of a certain row or a member of a certain column; the item is the same in the two cases, but its context is different.

If you will allow me a little undue simplicity I can go on to say rather more about neutral monism, but you must understand that I am taking more simply than I ought to do because there is not time to put in all the shadings and qualifications. I was talking a moment ago about the appearances that a chair presents. If we take any one of these chairs, we can all look at it, and it presents a different appearance to each of us. Taken all together, taking all the different appearances that that chair is presenting to all of us at this moment, you get something that belongs to physics. So that, if one takes sense-data and arranges together all those sense-data that appear to different people at a given moment and are such as we should ordinarily say are appearances of the same physical object, then that class of sense-data will give you something that belongs to physics, namely, the chair at this moment. On the other hand, if instead of taking all the appearances that that chair presents to all of us at this moment, I take all the appearances that the different chairs in this room present to me at this moment, I get quite another group of particulars. All the different appearances that different chairs present to me now will give you something belonging to psychology, because that will give you my experiences at the present moment. Broadly speaking, according to what one may take as an expansion of William James, that should be the definition of the difference between physics and psychology.

We commonly assume that there is a phenomenon which we call seeing the chair, but what I call my seeing the chair according to neutral monism is merely the existence of a certain particular, namely the particular which is the sense-datum of that chair at that moment. And I and the chair are both logical fictions, both being in fact a series of classes of particulars, of which one will be that particular which we call my seeing the chair. That actual appearance that the chair is presenting to me now is a member of me and a member of the chair, I and the chair being logical fictions. That will be at any rate a view that you can consider if you are engaged in vindicating neutral monism. There is no simple entity that you can point to and say: this entity is physical and not mental. According to William James and neutral monists that will not be the case with any simple entity that you may take. Any such entity will be a member of physical series and a member of mental series. Now I want to say that if you wish to test such a theory as that of neutral monism, if you wish to discover whether it is true or false, you cannot hope to get any distance with your problem unless you have at your fingers' ends the theory of logic that I have been talking of. You never can tell otherwise what can be done with a given material, whether you can concoct out of a given material the sort of logical fictions that will have the properties you want in psychology and in physics. That sort of thing is by no means easy to decide. You can only decide it if you really have a very considerable technical facility in these matters. Having said that, I ought to proceed to tell you that I have discovered whether neutral monism is true or not, because otherwise you may not believe that logic is any use in the matter. But I do not profess to know whether it is true or not. I feel more and more inclined to think that it may be true. I feel more and more that the difficulties that occur in regard to it are all of the sort that may be solved by ingenuity. But nevertheless there *are* a number of difficulties; there are a number of problems, some of which I have spoken about in the course of these lectures. One is the question of belief and the other sorts of facts involving two verbs. If there are such facts as this, that, I think, may make neutral monism rather difficult, but as I was pointing out, there is the theory that one calls behaviourism, which belongs logically with neutral monism, and that theory would altogether dispense with those facts containing two verbs, and would therefore dispose of that argument against neutral monism. There is, on the other hand, the argument from emphatic particulars, such as 'this' and 'now' and 'here' and such words as that, which are not very easy to reconcile, to my mind, with the view which does not distinguish between a particular and experiencing that particular. But the argument about emphatic particulars is so delicate and so subtle that I cannot feel quite sure whether it is a valid one or not, and I think the longer one pursues philosophy, the more conscious one becomes how extremely often one has been taken in by fallacies, and the less willing one is to be quite sure that an argument is valid if there is anything about it that is at all subtle or elusive, at all difficult to grasp. That makes me a little cautious and doubtful about all these arguments, and therefore although I am quite sure that the question of the truth or falsehood of neutral monism is not to be solved except by these means, yet I do not profess to know whether neutral monism is true or is not. I am not without hopes of finding out in the course of time, but I do not profess to know yet.

As I said earlier in this lecture, one thing that our technique does, is to give us a means of constructing a given body of symbolic propositions with the minimum of apparatus, and every diminution in apparatus diminishes the risk of error. Suppose, e.g., that you have constructed your physics with a certain number of entities and a certain number of premises; suppose you discover that by a little ingenuity you can dispense with half of those entities and half of those premises, you clearly have diminished the risk of error, because if you had before 10 entities and 10 premises, then the 5 you have now would be all right, but it is not true conversely that if the 5 you have now are all right, the 10 must have been. Therefore you diminish the risk of error with every diminution of entities and premises. When I spoke about the desk and said I was not going to assume the existence of a persistent substance underlying its appearances, it is an example of the case in point. You have anyhow the successive appearances, and if you can get on without assuming the metaphysical and constant desk, you have a smaller risk of error than you had before. You would not necessarily have a smaller risk of error if you were tied down to *denying* the metaphysical desk. That is the advantage of Occam's Razor, that it diminishes your risk of error. Considered in that way you may say that the whole of our problem belongs rather to science than to philosophy. I think perhaps that is true, but I believe the only difference between science and philosophy is, that science is what you more or less know and philosophy is what you do not know. Philosophy is that part of science which at present people choose to have opinions about, but which they have no knowledge about. Therefore every advance in knowledge robs philosophy of some problems which formerly it had, and if there is any truth, if there is any value in the kind of procedure of mathematical logic, it will follow that a number of problems which had belonged to philosophy will have ceased to belong to philosophy and will belong to science. And of course the moment they become soluble, they become to a large class of philosophical minds uninteresting, because to many of the people who like philosophy, the charm of it consists in the speculative freedom, in the fact that you can play with hypotheses. You can think out this or that which *may* be true, which is a very valuable exercise until you discover what *is* true; but when you discover what is true the whole fruitful play of fancy in that region is curtailed, and you will abandon that region and pass on. Just as there are families in America who from the time of the Pilgrim Fathers onward had always migrated westward, towards the backwoods, because they did not like civilized life, so the philosopher has an adventurous disposition and likes to dwell in the region where there are still uncertainties. It is true that the transferring of a region from philosophy into science will make it distasteful to a very important and useful type of mind. I think that is true of a good deal of the applications of mathematical logic in the directions that I have been indicating. It makes it dry, precise, methodical, and in that way robs it of a certain quality that it had when you could play with it more freely. I do not feel that it is my place to apologize for that, because if it is true, it is true. If it is not true, of course, I do owe you an apology; but if it is, it is not my fault, and therefore I do not feel I owe any apology for any sort of dryness or dullness in the world. I would say this too, that for those who have any taste for mathematics, for those who like symbolic constructions, that sort of world is a very delightful one, and if you do not find it otherwise attractive, all that is necessary to do is to acquire a taste for mathematics, and then you will have a very agreeable world, and with that conclusion I will bring this course of lectures to an end.

# 1924

# Logical Atomism

The philosophy which I advocate is generally regarded as a species of realism, and accused of inconsistency because of the elements in it which seem contrary to that doctrine. For my part, I do not regard the issue between realists and their opponents as a fundamental one; I could alter my view on this issue without changing my mind as to any of the doctrines upon which I wish to lay stress. I hold that logic is what is fundamental in philosophy, and that schools should be characterized rather by their logic than by their metaphysic. My own logic is atomic, and it is this aspect upon which I should wish to lay stress. Therefore I prefer to describe my philosophy as 'logical atomism', rather than as 'realism', whether with or without some prefixed adjective.

A few words as to historical development may be useful by way of preface. I came to philosophy through mathematics, or rather through the wish to find some reason to believe in the truth of mathematics. From early youth, I had an ardent desire to believe that there can be such a thing as knowledge, combined with a great difficulty in accepting much that passes as knowledge. It seemed clear that the best chance of finding indubitable truth would be in pure mathematics, yet some of Euclid's axioms were obviously doubtful, and the infinitesimal calculus, as I was taught it, was a mass of sophisms, which I could not bring myself to regard as anything else. I saw no reason to doubt the truth of arithmetic, but I did not then know that arithmetic can be made to embrace all traditional pure mathematics. At the age of eighteen I read Mill's *Logic*, but was profoundly dissatisfied with his reasons for accepting arithmetic and geometry. I had not read Hume, but it seemed to me that pure empiricism (which I was disposed to accept) must lead to scepticism rather than to Mill's support of received scientific doctrines. At Cambridge I read Kant and Hegel, as well as Mr. Bradley's *Logic*, which influenced me profoundly. For some years I was a disciple of Mr. Bradley, but about 1898 I changed my views, largely as a result of arguments with G. E. Moore. I could no longer believe that knowing makes any difference to what is known. Also I found myself driven to pluralism. Analysis of mathematical propositions persuaded me that they could not be explained as even partial truths unless one admitted pluralism and the reality of relations. An accident led me at this time to study Leibniz, and I came to the conclusion (subsequently confirmed by Couturat's masterly researches) that many of his most characteristic opinions were due to the purely logical doctrine that every proposition has a subject and a predicate. This doctrine is one which Leibniz shares with Spinoza, Hegel, and Mr. Bradley; it seemed to me that, if it is rejected, the whole foundation for the metaphysics of all these philosophers is shattered. I therefore returned to the problem which had originally led me to philosophy, namely, the foundations of mathematics, applying to it a new logic derived largely from Peano and Frege, which proved (at least, so I believe) far more fruitful than that of traditional philosophy.

In the first place, I found that many of the stock philosophical arguments about mathematics (derived in the main from Kant) had been rendered invalid by the progress of mathematics in the meanwhile. Non-Euclidean geometry had undermined the argument of the transcendental aesthetic. Weierstrass had shown that the differential and integral calculus do not require the conception of the infinitesimal, and that, therefore, all that had been said by philosophers on such subjects as the continuity of space and time and motion must be regarded as sheer error.

Cantor freed the conception of infinite number from contradiction, and thus disposed of Kant's antinomies as well
as many of Hegel's. Finally Frege showed in detail how
arithmetic can be deduced from pure logic, without the
need of any fresh ideas or axioms, thus disproving Kant's
assertion that '7 + 5 = 12' is synthetic—at least in the
obvious interpretation of that dictum. As all these results
were obtained, not by any heroic method, but by patient
detailed reasoning, I began to think it probable that philosophy had erred in adopting heroic remedies for intellectual
difficulties, and that solutions were to be found merely by
greater care and accuracy. This view I had come to hold
more and more strongly as time went on, and it has led
me to doubt whether philosophy, as a study distinct from
science and possessed of a method of its own, is anything
more than an unfortunate legacy from theology.

Frege's work was not final, in the first place because it
applied only to arithmetic, not to other branches of mathematics; in the second place because his premises did not
exclude certain contradictions to which all past systems of
formal logic turned out to be liable. Dr. Whitehead and I
in collaboration tried to remedy these two defects, in *Principia Mathematica,* which, however, still falls short of finality
in some fundamental points (notably the axiom of
reducibility). But in spite of its shortcomings I think that no
one who reads this book will dispute its main contention,
namely, that from certain ideas and axioms of formal
logic, by the help of the logic of relations, all pure mathematics can be deduced, without any new undefined idea
or unproved propositions. The technical methods of mathematical logic, as developed in this book, seem to me very
powerful, and capable of providing a new instrument for
the discussion of many problems that have hitherto remained subject to philosophic vagueness. Dr. Whitehead's
*Concept of Nature* and *Principles of Natural Knowledge* may
serve as an illustration of what I mean.

When pure mathematics is organized as a deductive
system—i.e. as the set of all those propositions that can be

deduced from an assigned set of premisses—it becomes
obvious that, if we are to believe in the truth of pure
mathematics, it cannot be solely because we believe in the
truth of the set of premisses. Some of the premisses are
much less obvious than some of their consequences, and
are believed chiefly because of their consequences. This
will be found to be always the case when a science is
arranged as a deductive system. It is not the logically simplest propositions of the system that are the most obvious,
or that provide the chief part of our reasons for believing
in the system. With the empirical sciences this is evident.
Electro-dynamics, for example, can be concentrated into
Maxwell's equations, but these equations are believed because of the observed truth of certain of their logical consequences. Exactly the same thing happens in the pure realm
of logic; the logically first principles of logic—at least some
of them—are to be believed, not on their own account, but
on account of their consequences. The epistemological question: 'Why should I believe this set of propositions?' is
quite different from the logical question: 'What is the smallest and logically simplest group of propositions from which
this set of propositions can be deduced?' Our reasons for
believing logic and pure mathematics are, in part, only
inductive and probable, in spite of the fact that, in their
*logical* order, the propositions of logic and pure mathematics follow from the premisses of logic by pure deduction.
I think this point important, since errors are liable to arise
from assimilating the logical to the epistemological order,
and also, conversely, from assimilating the epistemological
to the logical order. The only way in which work on mathematical logic throws light on the truth or falsehood of
mathematics is by disproving the supposed antinomies.
This shows that mathematics *may* be true. But to show that
mathematics *is* true would require other methods and other
considerations.

One very important heuristic maxim which Dr.
Whitehead and I found, by experience, to be applicable in
mathematical logic, and have since applied to various other

fields, is a form of Occam's Razor. When some set of supposed entities has neat logical properties, it turns out, in a great many instances, that the supposed entities can be replaced by purely logical structures composed of entities which have not such neat properties. In that case, in interpreting a body of propositions hitherto believed to be about the supposed entities, we can substitute the logical structures without altering any of the detail of the body of propositions in question. This is an economy, because entities with neat logical properties are always inferred, and if the propositions in which they occur can be interpreted without making this inference, the ground for the inference fails, and our body of propositions is secured against the need of a doubtful step. The principle may be stated in the form: 'Wherever possible, substitute constructions out of known entities for inferences to unknown entities.'

The uses of this principle are very various, but are not intelligible in detail to those who do not know mathematical logic. The first instance I came across was what I have called 'the principle of abstraction', or 'the principle which dispenses with abstraction'.[1] This principle is applicable in the case of any symmetrical and transitive relation, such as equality. We are apt to infer that such relations arise from possession of some common quality. This may or may not be true; probably it is true in some cases and not in others. But all the formal purposes of a common quality can be served by membership of the group of terms having the said relation to a given term. Take magnitude, for example. Let us suppose that we have a group of rods, all equally long. It is easy to suppose that there is a certain quality, called their length, which they all share. But all propositions in which this supposed quality occurs will retain their truth-value unchanged if, instead of 'length of the rod $x$' we take 'membership of the group of all those rods which are as long as $x$'. In various special cases—e.g.

---

[1] *External World*, p. 42.

the definition of real numbers—a simpler construction is possible.

A very important example of the principle is Frege's definition of the cardinal number of a given set of terms as the class of all sets that are 'similar' to the given set— where two sets are 'similar' when there is a one-one relation whose domain is the one set and whose converse domain is the other. Thus a cardinal number is the class of all those classes which are similar to a given class. This definition leaves unchanged the truth-values of all propositions in which cardinal numbers occur, and avoids the inference to a set of entities called 'cardinal numbers', which were never needed except for the purpose of making arithmetic intelligible, and are now no longer needed for that purpose.

Perhaps even more important is the fact that classes themselves can be dispensed with by similar methods. Mathematics is full of propositions which seem to require that a class or an aggregate should be in some sense a single entity—e.g. the proposition 'the number of combinations of $n$ things any number at a time is $2^n$'. Since $2^n$ is always greater than $n$, this proposition leads to difficulties if classes are admitted because the number of classes of entities in the universe is greater than the number of entities in the universe, which would be odd if classes were some among entities. Fortunately, all the propositions in which classes appear to be mentioned can be interpreted without supposing that there are classes. This is perhaps the most important of all the applications of our principle. (See *Principia Mathematica*, *20.)

Another important example concerns what I call 'definite descriptions', i.e. such phrases as 'the even prime', 'the present King of England', 'the present King of France'. There has always been a difficulty in interpreting such propositions as 'the present King of France does not exist'. The difficulty arose through supposing that 'the present King of France' is the subject of this proposition, which made it necessary to suppose that he subsists although he

does not exist. But it is difficult to attribute even subsistence to 'the round square' or 'the even prime greater than
2'. In fact, 'the round square does not subsist' is just as true
as 'the present King of France does not exist'. Thus the
distinction between existence and subsistence does not
help us. The fact is that, when the words 'the so-and-so'
occur in a proposition, there is no corresponding single
constituent of the proposition, and when the proposition
is fully analysed the words 'the so-and-so' have disappeared. An important consequence of the theory of descriptions is that it is meaningless to say 'A exists' unless
'A' is (or stands for) a phrase of the form 'the so-and-so'.
If the so-and-so exists, and $x$ is the so-and-so, to say '$x$
exists' is nonsense. Existence, in the sense in which it is
ascribed to single entities, is thus removed altogether from
the list of fundamentals. The ontological argument and
most of its refutations are found to depend upon bad
grammar. (See *Principia Mathematica,* *14.)

There are many other examples of the substitution of
constructions for inferences in pure mathematics, for example, series, ordinal numbers, and real numbers. But I
will pass on to the examples in physics.

Points and instants are obvious examples: Dr. Whitehead has shown how to construct them out of sets of
events all of which have a finite extent and a finite duration. In relativity theory, it is not points or instants that we
primarily need, but event-particles, which correspond to
what, in older language, might be described as a point at
an instant, or an instantaneous point. (In former days, a
point of space endured throughout all time, and an instant
of time pervaded all space. Now the unit that mathematical
physics wants has neither spatial nor temporal extension.)
Event-particles are constructed by just the same logical
process by which points and instants were constructed. In
such constructions, however, we are on a different plane
from that of constructions in pure mathematics. The possibility of constructing an event-particle depends upon the
existence of sets of events with certain properties; whether

the required events exist can only be known empirically, if at all. There is therefore no *a priori* reason to expect continuity (in the mathematical sense), or to feel confident that event-particles can be constructed. If the quantum theory should seem to demand a discrete space-time, our logic is just as ready to meet its requirements as to meet those of traditional physics, which demands continuity. The question is purely empirical, and our logic is (as it ought to be) equally adapted to either alternative.

Similar considerations apply to a particle of matter, or to a piece of matter of finite size. Matter, traditionally, has two of those 'neat' properties which are the mark of a logical construction; first, that two pieces of matter cannot be at the same place at the same time; secondly, that one piece of matter cannot be in two places at the same time. Experience in the substitution of constructions for inferences makes one suspicious of anything so tidy and exact. One cannot help feeling that impenetrability is not an empirical fact, derived from observation of billiard-balls, but is something logically necessary. This feeling is wholly justified, but it could not be so if matter were not a logical construction. An immense number of occurrences coexist in any little region of space-time; when we are speaking of what is not logical construction, we find no such property as impenetrability, but, on the contrary, endless overlapping of the events in a part of space-time, however small. The reason that matter is impenetrable is because our definitions make it so. Speaking roughly, and merely so as to give a notion of how this happens, we may say that a piece of matter is all that happens in a certain track in space-time, and that we construct the tracks called bits of matter in such a way that they do not intersect. Matter is impenetrable because it is easier to state the laws of physics if we make our constructions so as to secure impenetrability. Impenetrability is a logically necessary result of definition, though the fact that such a definition is convenient is empirical. Bits of matter are not among the bricks out of which the world is built. The bricks are events, and bits of matter are portions of the structure to which we find it convenient to give separate attention.

In the philosophy of mental occurrences there are also opportunities for the application of our principle of constructions *versus* inferences. The subject, and the relation of a cognition to what is known, both have that schematic quality that arouses our suspicions. It is clear that the subject, if it is to be preserved at all, must be preserved as a construction, not as an inferred entity; the only question is whether the subject is sufficiently useful to be worth constructing. The relation of a cognition to what is known, again, cannot be a straightforward single ultimate, as I at one time believed it to be. Although I do not agree with pragmatism, I think William James was right in drawing attention to the complexity of 'knowing'. It is impossible in a general summary, such as the present, to set out the reasons for this view. But whoever has acquiesced in our principle will agree that here is prima facie a case for applying it. Most of my *Analysis of Mind* consists of applications of this principle. But as psychology is scientifically much less perfected than physics, the opportunities for applying the principle are not so good. The principle depends, for its use, upon the existence of some fairly reliable body of propositions, which are to be interpreted by the logician in such a way as to preserve their truth while minimizing the element of inference to unobserved entities. The principle therefore presupposes a moderately advanced science, in the absence of which the logician does not know what he ought to construct. Until recently, it would have seemed necessary to construct geometrical points; now it is event-particles that are wanted. In view of such a change in an advanced subject like physics, it is clear that constructions in psychology must be purely provisional.

I have been speaking hitherto of what it is *not* necessary to assume as part of the ultimate constituents of the world. But logical constructions, like all other constructions, require materials, and it is time to turn to the positive question, as to what these materials are to be. This question, however, requires as a preliminary a discussion of logic and language and their relation to what they try to represent.

The influence of language on philosophy has, I believe, been profound and almost unrecognized. If we are not to be misled by this influence, it is necessary to become conscious of it, and to ask ourselves deliberately how far it is legitimate. The subject-predicate logic, with the substance-attribute metaphysic, are a case in point. It is doubtful whether either would have been invented by people speaking a non-Aryan language; certainly they do not seem to have arisen in China, except in connection with Buddhism, which brought Indian philosophy with it. Again, it is natural, to take a different kind of instance, to suppose that a proper name which can be used significantly stands for a single entity; we suppose that there is a certain more or less persistent being called 'Socrates', because the same name is applied to a series of occurrences which we are led to regard as appearances of this one being. As language grows more abstract, a new set of entities come into philosophy, namely, those represented by abstract words—the universals. I do not wish to maintain that there are no universals, but certainly there are many abstract words which do not stand for single universals—e.g. triangularity and rationality. In these respects language misleads us both by its vocabulary and by its syntax. We must be on our guard in both respects if our logic is not to lead to a false metaphysic.

Syntax and vocabulary have had different kinds of effects on philosophy. Vocabulary has most influence on common sense. It might be urged, conversely, that common sense produces our vocabulary. This is only partially true. A word is applied at first to things which are more or less similar, without any reflection as to whether they have any point of identity. But when once usage has fixed the objects to which the word is to be applied, common sense is influenced by the existence of the word, and tends to

suppose that one word must stand for one object, which
will be a universal in the case of an adjective or an abstract
word. Thus the influence of vocabulary is towards a kind
of platonic pluralism of things and ideas.

The influence of syntax, in the case of the Indo-Europe-
an languages, is quite different. Almost any proposition
can be put into a form in which it has a subject and a
predicate, united by a copula. It is natural to infer that
every fact has a corresponding form, and consists in the
possession of a quality by a substance. This leads, of course,
to monism, since the fact that there were several substances (if it were a fact) would not have the requisite form.
Philosophers, as a rule, believe themselves free from this
sort of influence of linguistic forms, but most of them seem
to me to be mistaken in this belief. In thinking about
abstract matters, the fact that the words for abstractions
are no more abstract than ordinary words always makes
it easier to think about the words than about what they
stand for, and it is almost impossible to resist consistently
the temptation to think about the words.

Those who do not succumb to the subject-predicate
logic are apt to get only one step further, and admit relations of two terms, such as before-and-after, greater-and-
less, right-and-left. Language lends itself to this extension
of the subject-predicate logic, since we say '*A* precedes *B*',
'*A* exceeds *B*', and so on. It is easy to prove that the fact
expressed by a proposition of this sort cannot consist of
the possession of a quality by a substance, or of the possession of two or more qualities by two or more substances.
(See *Principles of Mathematics,* §214.) The extension of the
subject-predicate logic is therefore right so far as it goes,
but obviously a further extension can be proved necessary
by exactly similar arguments. How far it is necessary to go
up the series of three-term, four-term, five-term . . . relations I do not know. But it is certainly necessary to go
beyond two-term relations. In projective geometry, for
example, the order of points on a line or of planes through
a line requires a four-term relation.

A very unfortunate effect of the peculiarities of language is in connection with adjectives and relations. All words are of the same logical type; a word is a class of series, of noises or shapes according as it is heard or read. But the meanings of words are of various different types; an attribute (expressed by an adjective) is of a different type from the objects to which it can be (whether truly or falsely) attributed; a relation (expressed perhaps by a preposition, perhaps by a transitive verb, perhaps in some other way) is of a different type from the terms between which it holds or does not hold. The definition of a logical type is as follows: *A* and *B* are of the same logical type if, and only if, given any fact of which *A* is a constituent, there is a corresponding fact which has *B* as a constituent, which either results by substituting *B* for *A,* or is the negation of what so results. To take an illustration, Socrates and Aristotle are of the same type, because 'Socrates was a philosopher' and 'Aristotle was a philosopher' are both facts; Socrates and Caligula are of the same type, because 'Socrates was a philosopher' and 'Caligula was not a philosopher' are both facts. To love and to kill are of the same type, because 'Plato loved Socrates' and 'Plato did not kill Socrates' are both facts. It follows formally from the definition that, when two words have meanings of different types, the relations of the words to what they mean are of different types; that is to say, there is not one relation of meaning between words and what they stand for, but as many relations of meaning, each of a different logical type, as there are logical types among the objects for which there are words. This fact is a very potent source of error and confusion in philosophy. In particular, it has made it extraordinarily difficult to express in words any theory of relations which is logically capable of being true, because language cannot preserve the difference of type between a relation and its terms. Most of the arguments for and against the reality of relations have been vitiated through this source of confusion.

At this point, I propose to digress for a moment, and

to say, as shortly as I can, what I believe about relations. My own views on the subject of relations in the past were less clear than I thought them, but were by no means the views which my critics supposed them to be. Owing to lack of clearness in my own thoughts, I was unable to convey my meaning. The subject of relations is difficult, and I am far from claiming to be now clear about it. But I think certain points are clear to me. At the time when I wrote *The Principles of Mathematics,* I had not yet seen the necessity of logical types. The doctrine of types profoundly affects logic, and I think shows what, exactly, is the valid element in the arguments of those who oppose 'external' relations. But so far from strengthening their main position, the doctrine of types leads, on the contrary, to a more complete and radical atomism than any that I conceived to be possible twenty years ago. The question of relations is one of the most important that arise in philosophy, as most other issues turn on it: monism and pluralism; the question whether anything is wholly true except the whole of truth, or wholly real except the whole of reality; idealism and realism, in some of their forms; perhaps the very existence of philosophy as a subject distinct from science and possessing a method of its own. It will serve to make my meaning clear if I take a passage in Mr. Bradley's *Essays on Truth and Reality,* not for controversial purposes, but because it raises exactly the issues that ought to be raised. But first of all I will try to state my own view, without argument.[2]

Certain contradictions—of which the simplest and oldest is the one about Epimenides the Cretan, who said that all Cretans were liars, which may be reduced to the man who says 'I am lying'—convinced me, after five years devoted mainly to this one question, that no solution is technically possible without the doctrine of types. In its technical

---

[2]I am much indebted to my friend Wittgenstein in this matter. See his *Tractatus Logico-Philosophicus,* Kegan Paul, 1922. I do not accept all his doctrines, but my debt to him will be obvious to those who read his book.

form, this doctrine states merely that a word or symbol may form part of a significant proposition, and in this sense have meaning, without being always able to be substituted for another word or symbol in the same or some other proposition without producing nonsense. Stated in this way, the doctrine may seem like a truism. 'Brutus killed Caesar' is significant, but 'Killed killed Caesar' is nonsense, so that we cannot replace 'Brutus' by 'killed', although both words have meaning. This is plain common sense, but unfortunately almost all philosophy consists in an attempt to forget it. The following words, for example, by their very nature, sin against it: attribute, relation, complex, fact, truth, falsehood, not, liar, omniscience. To give a meaning to these words, we have to make a detour by way of words or symbols and the different ways in which they may mean; and even then, we usually arrive, not at one meaning, but at an infinite series of different meanings. Words, as we saw, are all of the same logical type; therefore when the meanings of two words are of different types, the relations of the two words to what they stand for are also of different types. Attribute-words and relation-words are of the same type, therefore we can say significantly 'attribute-words and relation-words have different uses'. But we cannot say significantly 'attributes are not relations'. By our definition of types, since relations are relations, the form of words 'attributes are relations' must be not false, but meaningless, and the form of words 'attributes are not relations', similarly must be not true, but meaningless. Nevertheless, the statement 'attribute-words are not relation-words' is significant and true.

We can now tackle the question of internal and external relations, remembering that the usual formulations, on both sides, are inconsistent with the doctrine of types. I will begin with attempts to state the doctrine of external relations. It is useless to say 'terms are independent of their relations', because 'independent' is a word which means nothing. Two events may be said to be causally independent when no causal chain leads from one to the other; this

happens, in the special theory of relativity, when the sepa-
ration between the events is space-like. Obviously this sense
of 'independent' is irrelevant. If, when we say 'terms are
independent of their relations', we mean 'two terms which
have a given relation would be the same if they did not
have it', that is obviously false; for, being what they are,
they have the relation, and therefore whatever does not
have the relation is different. If we mean—as opponents
of external relations suppose us to mean—that the relation
is a third term which comes between the other two terms
and is somehow hooked on to them, that is obviously
absurd, for in that case the relation has ceased to be a
relation, and all that is truly relational is the hooking of the
relation to the terms. The conception of the relation as a
third term between the other two sins against the doctrine
of types, and must be avoided with the utmost care.

What, then, can we mean by the doctrine of external
relations? Primarily this, that a relational proposition is
not, in general, logically equivalent formally to one or
more subject-predicate propositions. Stated more precisely: Given a relational propositional function '$xRy$', it is not
in general the case that we find predicates $\alpha$, $\beta$, $\gamma$, such
that, for all values of $x$ and $y$, $xRy$ is equivalent to $x\alpha$, $y\beta$,
$(x,y)\gamma$ (where $(x, y)$ stands for the whole consisting of $x$ and
$y$), or to any one or two of these. This, and this only, is what
I mean to affirm when I assert the doctrine of external
relations; and this, clearly, is at least part of what Mr.
Bradley denies when he asserts the doctrine of internal
relations.

In place of 'unities' or 'complexes', I prefer to speak of
'facts'. It must be understood that the word 'fact' cannot
occur significantly in any position in a sentence where the
word 'simple' can occur significantly, nor can a fact occur
where a simple can occur. We must not say 'facts are not
simples'. We can say, 'The symbol for a fact must not
replace the symbol for a simple, or vice versa, if significance
is to be preserved.' But it should be observed that, in this
sentence, the word 'for' has different meanings on the two

occasions of its use. If we are to have a language which is to safeguard us from errors as to types, the symbol for a fact must be a proposition, not a single word or letter. Facts can be asserted or denied, but cannot be named. (When I say 'facts cannot be named', this is, strictly speaking, nonsense. What can be said without falling into nonsense is: 'The symbol for a fact is not a name.') This illustrates how meaning is a different relation for different types. The way to mean a fact is to assert it; the way to mean a simple is to name it. Obviously naming is different from asserting and similar differences exist where more advanced types are concerned, though language has no means of expressing the differences.

There are many other matters in Mr. Bradley's examination of my views which call for reply. But as my present purpose is explanatory rather than controversial, I will pass them by, having, I hope, already said enough on the question of relations and complexes to make it clear what is the theory that I advocate. I will only add, as regards the doctrine of types, that most philosophers assume it now and then, and few would deny it, but that all (so far as I know) avoid formulating it precisely or drawing from it those deductions that are inconvenient for their systems.

I come now to some of Mr. Bradley's criticism (*loc. cit.,* pp. 280 ff.). He says:

'Mr. Russell's main position has remained to myself incomprehensible. On the one side I am led to think that he defends a strict pluralism, for which nothing is admissible beyond simple terms and external relations. On the other side Mr. Russell seems to assert emphatically, and to use throughout, ideas which such a pluralism surely must repudiate. He throughout stands upon unities which are complex and which cannot be analysed into terms and relations. These two positions to my mind are irreconcilable, since the second, as I understand it, contradicts the first flatly.'

With regard to external relations, my view is the one I have just stated, not the one commonly imputed by those who disagree. But with regard to unities, the question is more difficult. The topic is one with which language, by its very nature, is peculiarly unfitted to deal. I must beg the reader, therefore, to be indulgent if what I say is not exactly what I mean, and to try to see what I mean in spite of unavoidable linguistic obstacles to clear expression.

To begin with, I do not believe that there are complexes or unities in the same sense in which there are simples. I did believe this when I wrote *The Principles of Mathematics,* but, on account of the doctrine of types, I have since abandoned this view. To speak loosely, I regard simples and complexes as always of different types. That is to say, the statements 'There are simples' and 'There are complexes' use the words 'there are' in different senses. But if I use the words 'there are' in the sense which they have in the statement 'there are simples', then the form of words 'there are not complexes' is neither true nor false, but meaningless. This shows how difficult it is to say clearly, in ordinary language, what I want to say about complexes. In the language of mathematical logic it is much easier to say what I want to say, but much harder to induce people to understand what I mean when I say it.

When I speak of 'simples', I ought to explain that I am speaking of something not experienced as such, but known only inferentially as the limit of analysis. It is quite possible that, by greater logical skill, the need for assuming them could be avoided. A logical language will not lead to error if its simple symbols (i.e. those not having any parts that are symbols, or any significant structure) all stand for objects of some one type, even if these objects are not simple. The only drawback to such a language is that it is incapable of dealing with anything simpler than the objects which it represents by simple symbols. But I confess it seems obvious to me (as it did to Leibniz) that what is complex must be composed of simples, though the number of constituents may be infinite. It is also obvious that the logical uses of the old notion of substance (i.e. those uses which do not imply temporal duration) can only be applied, if at all, to simples; objects of other types do not have that kind of being which one associates with substances. The essence of a substance, from the symbolic point of view, is that it can only be named—in old-fashioned language, it never occurs in a proposition except as the subject or as one of the terms of a relation. If what we take to be simple is really complex, we may get into trouble by naming it, when what we ought to do is to assert it. For example, if Plato loves Socrates, there is not an entity 'Plato's love for Socrates', but only the fact that Plato loves Socrates. And in speaking of this as 'a fact', we are already making it more substantial and more of a unity than we have any right to do.

Attributes and relations, though they may be not susceptible of analysis, differ from substances by the fact that they suggest a structure, and that there can be no significant symbol which symbolizes them in isolation. All propositions in which an attribute or a relation *seems* to be the subject are only significant if they can be brought into a form in which the attribute is attributed or the relation relates. If this were not the case, there would be significant propositions in which an attribute or a relation would occupy a position appropriate to a substance, which would be contrary to the doctrine of types, and would produce contradictions. Thus the proper symbol for 'yellow' (assuming for the sake of illustration that this is an attribute) is not the single word 'yellow', but the propositional function '$x$ is yellow', where the structure of the symbol shows the position which the word 'yellow' must have if it is to be significant. Similarly the relation 'precedes' must not be represented by this one word, but by the symbol '$x$ precedes $y$', showing the way in which the symbol can occur significantly. (It is here assumed that values are not assigned to $x$ and $y$ when we are speaking of the attribute or relation itself.)

The symbol for the simplest possible kind of fact will still be of the form '$x$ is yellow' or '$x$ precedes $y$', only that '$x$' and '$y$' will be no longer undetermined variables, but names.

In addition to the fact that we do not experience simples as such, there is another obstacle to the actual creation
of a correct logical language such as I have been trying to
describe. This obstacle is vagueness. All our words are
more or less infected with vagueness, by which I mean that
is not always clear whether they apply to a given object or
not. It is of the nature of words to be more or less general,
and not to apply only to a single particular, but that would
not make them vague if the particulars to which they
applied were a definite set. But this is never the case in
practice. The defect, however, is one which it is easy to
imagine removed, however difficult it may be to remove
it in fact.

The purpose of the foregoing discussion of an ideal
logical language (which would of course be wholly useless
for daily life) is twofold: first, to prevent inferences from
the nature of language to the nature of the world, which
are fallacious because they depend upon the logical defects
of language; secondly, to suggest, by inquiring what logic
requires of a language which is to avoid contradiction,
what sort of a structure we may reasonably suppose the
world to have. If I am right, there is nothing in logic that
can help us to decide between monism and pluralism, or
between the view that there are ultimate relational facts
and the view that there are none. My own decision in
favour of pluralism and relations is taken on empirical
grounds, after convincing myself that the *a priori* arguments to the contrary are invalid. But I do not think these
arguments can be adequately refuted without a thorough
treatment of logical types, of which the above is a mere
sketch.

This brings me, however, to a question of method
which I believe to be very important. What are we to take
as data in philosophy? What shall we regard as having the
greatest likelihood of being true, and what as proper to be
rejected if it conflicts with other evidence? It seems to me
that science has a much greater likelihood of being true in
the main than any philosophy hitherto advanced (I do not,

of course, except my own). In science there are many matters about which people are agreed; in philosophy there are none. Therefore, although each proposition in a science may be false, and it is practically certain that there are some that are false, yet we shall be wise to build our philosophy upon science, because the risk of error in philosophy is pretty sure to be greater than in science. If we could hope for certainty in philosophy the matter would be otherwise, but so far as I can see such a hope would be a chimerical.

Of course those philosophers whose theories, prima facie, run counter to science always profess to be able to interpret science so that it shall remain true on its own level, with that minor degree of truth which ought to content the humble scientist. Those who maintain a position of this sort are bound—so it seems to me—to show in detail how the interpretation is to be effected. In many cases, I believe that this would be quite impossible. I do not believe, for instance, that those who disbelieve in the reality of relations (in some such sense as that explained above) can possibly interpret those numerous parts of science which employ asymmetrical relations. Even if I could see no way of answering the objections to relations raised (for example) by Mr. Bradley, I should still think it more likely than not that some answer was possible, because I should think an error in a very subtle and abstract argument more probable than so fundamental a falsehood in science. Admitting that everything we believe ourselves to know is doubtful, it seems, nevertheless, that what we believe ourselves to know in philosophy is more doubtful than the detail of science, though perhaps not more doubtful than its most sweeping generalizations.

The question of interpretation is of importance for almost every philosophy, and I am not at all inclined to deny that many scientific results require interpretation before they can be fitted into a coherent philosophy. The maxim of 'constructions *versus* inferences' is itself a maxim of interpretation. But I think that any valid kind of interpretation ought to leave the detail unchanged, though it may give a new meaning to fundamental ideas. In practice, this means that *structure* must be preserved. And a test of this is that all the propositions of a science should remain, though new meanings may be found for their terms. A case in point, on a nonphilosophical level, is the relation of the physical theory of light to our perceptions of colour. This provides different physical occurrences corresponding to different seen colours, and thus makes the structure of the physical spectrum the same as that of what we see when we look at a rainbow. Unless structure is preserved, we cannot validly speak of an interpretation. And structure is just what is destroyed by a monistic logic.

I do not mean, of course, to suggest that, in any region of science, the structure revealed at present by observation is exactly that which actually exists. On the contrary, it is in the highest degree probable that the actual structure is more fine-grained than the observed structure. This applies just as much to psychological as to physical material. It rests upon the fact that, where we perceive a difference (e.g. between two shades of colour), there is a difference, but where we do not perceive a difference it does not follow that there is not a difference. We have therefore a right, in all interpretation, to demand the preservation of observed differences, and the provision of room for hitherto unobserved differences, although we cannot say in advance what they will be, except when they can be inferentially connected with observed differences.

In science, structure is the main study. A large part of the importance of relativity comes from the fact that it has substituted a single four-dimensional manifold (space-time) for the two manifolds, three-dimensional space and one-dimensional time. This is a change of structure, and therefore has far-reaching consequences, but any change which does not involve a change of structure does not make much difference. The mathematical definition and study of structure (under the name of 'relation-numbers') form Part IV of *Principia Mathematica*.

The business of philosophy, as I conceive it, is essentially that of logical analysis, followed by logical synthesis.
Philosophy is more concerned than any special science
with relations of different sciences and possible conflicts
between them; in particular, it cannot acquiesce in a conflict
between physics and psychology, or between psychology
and logic. Philosophy should be comprehensive, and should
be bold in suggesting hypotheses as to the universe which
science is not yet in a position to confirm or confute. But
these should always be presented *as* hypotheses, not (as is
too often done) as immutable certainties like the dogmas
of religion. Although, moreover, comprehensive construction is part of the business of philosophy, I do not believe
it is the most important part. The most important part, to
my mind, consists in criticizing and clarifying notions which
are apt to be regarded as fundamental and accepted uncri-
tically. As instances I might mention: mind, matter, consciousness, knowledge, experience, causality, will, time. I
believe all these notions to be inexact and approximate,
essentially infected with vagueness, incapable of forming
part of any exact science. Out of the original manifold of
events, logical structures can be built which will have properties sufficiently like those of the above common notions
to account for their prevalence, but sufficiently unlike to
allow a great deal of error to creep in through their accept-
ance as fundamental.

I suggest the following as an outline of a possible structure of the world; it is no more than an outline, and is not
offered as more than possible.

The world consists of a number, perhaps finite, perhaps infinite, of entities which have various relations to
each other, and perhaps also various qualities. Each of
these entities may be called an 'event'; from the point of
view of old-fashioned physics, an event occupies a short
finite time and a small finite amount of space, but as we
are not going to have an old-fashioned space and an old-
fashioned time, this statement cannot be taken at its face
value. Every event has to a certain number of others a

relation which may be called 'compresence'; from the point of view of physics, a collection of compresent events all occupy one small region in space-time. One example of a set of compresent events is what would be called the contents of one man's mind at one time—i.e. all his sensations, images, memories, thoughts, etc., which can coexist temporally. His visual field has, in one sense, spatial extension, but this must not be confused with the extension of physical space-time; every part of his visual field is compresent with every other part, and with the rest of 'the contents of his mind' at that time, and a collection of compresent events occupies a minimal region in space-time. There are such collections not only where there are brains, but everywhere. At any point in 'empty space', a number of stars could be photographed if a camera were introduced; we believe that light travels over the regions intermediate between its source and our eyes, and therefore something is happening in these regions. If light from a number of different sources reaches a certain minimal region in space-time, then at least one event corresponding to each of these sources exists in this minimal region, and all these events are compresent.

We will define a set of compresent events as a 'minimal region'. We find that minimal regions form a four-dimensional manifold, and that, by a little logical manipulation, we can construct from them the manifold of space-time that physics requires. We find also that, from a number of different minimal regions, we can often pick out a set of events, one from each, which are closely similar when they come from neighbouring regions, and vary from one region to another according to discoverable laws. These are the laws of the propagation of light, sound, etc. We find also that certain regions in space-time have quite peculiar properties; these are the regions which are said to be occupied by 'matter'. Such regions can be collected, by means of the laws of physics, into tracks or tubes, very much more extended in one dimension of space-time than in the other three. Such a tube constitutes the 'history' of a piece of matter; from the point of view of the piece of matter itself, the dimension in which it is most extended can be called 'time', but it is only the private time of that piece of matter, because it does not correspond exactly with the dimension in which another piece of matter is most extended. Not only is space-time very peculiar within a piece of matter, but it is also rather peculiar in its neighbourhood, growing less so as the spatio-temporal distance grows greater; the law of this peculiarity is the law of gravitation.

All kinds of matter to some extent, but some kinds of matter (viz. nervous tissue) more particularly, are liable to form 'habits', i.e. to alter their structure in a given environment in such a way that, when they are subsequently in a similar environment, they reacts in a new way, but if similar environments recur often, the reaction in the end becomes nearly uniform, while remaining different from the reaction on the first occasion. (When I speak of the reaction of a piece of matter to its environment, I am thinking both of the constitution of the set of compresent events of which it consists, and of the nature of the track in space-time which constitutes what we should ordinarily call its motion; these are called a 'reaction to the environment' in so far as there are laws correlating them with characteristics of the environment.) Out of habit, the peculiarities of what we call 'mind' can be constructed; a mind is a track of sets of compresent events in a region of space-time where there is matter which is peculiarly liable to form habits. The greater the liability, the more complex and organized the mind becomes. Thus a mind and a brain are not really distinct, but when we speak of a mind we are thinking chiefly of the set of compresent events in the region concerned, and of their several relations to other events forming parts of other periods in the history of the spatio-temporal tube which we are considering, whereas when we speak of a brain we are taking the set of compresent events as a whole, and considering its external relations to other sets of compresent events, also taken as wholes; in a word, 'we are considering the shape of the tube, not the events of which each cross-section of it is composed.

The above summary hypothesis would, of course, need to be amplified and refined in many ways in order to fit in completely with scientific facts. It is not put forward as a finished theory, but merely as a suggestion of the kind of thing that may be true. It is of course easy to imagine other hypotheses which may be true, for example, the hypothesis that there is nothing outside the series of sets of events constituting my history. I do not believe that there is any method of arriving at one sole possible hypothesis, and therefore certainty in metaphysics seems to me unattainable. In this respect I must admit that many other philosophies have the advantage, since in spite of their differences *inter se,* each arrives at certainty of its own exclusive truth.

# Bibliography

## PART ONE

*Selections from Russell's writings, grouped under headings which also appear in the index in bold type. The works to which references are made are given abbreviated titles, and the key to the abbreviations is given at the end of this part of the bibliography.*

| | |
|---|---|
| Atomism, logical: | I.M.T. Ch. XIX: M.PH.D. Ch. X, Ch. XVIII, § i. |
| Belief: | O.N.T. and F: O.KN.E.W. Ch. II: O.P: A.M. Ch. XII: I.M.T. Ch. XIX: H.KN.S.L. Pt. II, Ch. V. |
| Classes: | P. of M. Ch. VI: P. M. Introduction Ch. III and Introduction to 2nd Edition: I.M.PH. Ch. XVII. |
| Constructions, logical: | R.S–D.PH: O.KN.E.W. Ch. IV. |
| Descriptions, ambiguous: | P. of M. Ch. V: I.M.PH. Ch. XVI. |
| Descriptions, definite: | P. of M. Ch. V: O.D: P.M. Introduction Ch.I, Ch. III: I.M.PH. Ch. XVI: M.PH.D. Ch. VII, Ch. XVIII, § iii. |
| Facts: | O.KN.E.W. Ch. II: O.P: H.KN.S.L. Pt. II, Ch. XI. |
| Fictions, logical: | R.S–D. PH: O.KN.E.W. Ch. IV. |
| Functions, propositional: | P. of M. Ch. VII: P.M. Introduction Ch. I, Ch. II: I.M.PH. Ch. XV. |
| Knowledge, by acquaintance: | O.D: P. of PH. Ch. V: KN.A.KN.D: O.N.A. |
| Knowledge, by description: | O.D: P. of PH. Ch. V: KN.A.KN.D. |
| Monism, neutral: | O.N.A: A.M. Chs. V–VIII: M.PH.D. Ch. XII. |
| Names: | P. of M. Ch. IV: KN.A.KN.D: O.N.A: I.M.T. Ch. VI and Ch. VII: H.KN.S.L. Pt. II, Ch. III and Ch. IV: M.PH.D. Ch. XIV. |
| Numbers: | P. of M. Ch. XI: M.L.T.T: I.M.PH. Ch. I and Ch. II: M.PH. D. Ch. VIII. |
| Particulars: | P. of M. Ch. IV: R.U.P: H.KN.S.L. Pt. II, Ch. VIII: M.PH.D. Ch. XIV. |
| Perception: | P. of PH. Ch. V: U.C.M: R.S–D.PH: O.KN.E.W. Ch. IV: A.M. Chs. V–VIII: I.M.T. Ch. VIII and Ch. XI: H.KN.S.L. Pt. III: M.PH.D. Ch. II, Ch. IX, Ch. XI. |
| Pluralism: | O.N.T. and F: M.TH. of T: PH. of L. Ch. IV: M.PH.D. Ch. V. |

| | |
|---|---|
| Propositions: | O.P: I.M.T. Ch. XIII. |
| atomic: | P.M. Introduction to 2nd Edition: O.KN.E.W. Ch. II: I.M.T. Ch. XIX. |
| general: | P. of M. Ch. V: M.L.T.T: P.M. Introduction Ch. II and Introduction to 2nd Edition: H.KN.S.L. Pt. II, Ch. X. |
| logical: | P. of Phil. Chs. VIII–XI: I.M.PH. Ch. XVIII. |
| molecular: | P.M. Introduction to 2nd Edition: O.KN.E.W. Ch. II: I.M.T. Ch. XIX. |
| constituents of: | O.D: P. of PH. Ch. V: KN.A.KN.D. |
| Relations: | P. of M. Ch. IV and Ch. IX: P.M. Introduction Ch. III: M.TH. of T: O.KN.E.W. Ch. II: I.M.PH. Ch. V: M.PH.D. Ch. V. |
| Symbols, incomplete: | P.M. introduction Ch. III. |
| Truth: | P. of PH. Ch. XII: P.M. Introduction Ch. II: M.TH. of T: O.N.T. and F: O.P: A.M. Ch. XIII: I.M.T. Ch. X, Ch. XVI, Ch. XVII, Ch. XXI: H.KN.S.L. Pt. II, Chs. VIII–XI: M.PH.D. Ch. XV. |
| Types, theory of: | P. of M. Appendix B: M.L.T.T: P.M. Introduction Ch. II: I.M.PH. Ch. XIII: M. PH.D. Ch. VII. |
| Universals: | R.U.P: P. of PH. Chs. IX and X: I.M.T. Ch. XXV: M.PH.D. Ch. IV. |

## KEY TO ABBREVIATIONS

| | |
|---|---|
| A.M. | *The Analysis of Mind,* Allen and Unwin, first published 1921. |
| H.KN.S.L. | *Human Knowledge, its Scope and Limits,* Allen and Unwin, first published 1948. |
| I.M.PH. | *Introduction to Mathematical Philosophy,* Allen and Unwin, first published 1919. |
| I.M.T. | *An Inquiry into Meaning and Truth,* Allen and Unwin, first published in 1940. Reprinted by Penguin Books 1970. |
| KN.A.KN.D. | 'Knowledge by Acquaintance and Knowledge by Description', *Proceedings of the Aristotelian Society 1910-1911,* reprinted in *Mysticism and Logic,* which was first published by Longmans, Green 1918. Reprinted by Allen and Unwin 1929. |
| M.L.T.T. | 'Mathematical Logic as based on the Theory of Types', *American Journal of Mathematics,* 1908, reprinted in *Logic and Knowledge,* edited R. C. Marsh, Allen and Unwin, first published 1956. |
| M.PH.D. | *My Philosophical Development,* Allen and Unwin, first published 1959. |
| M.TH. of T. | *The Monistic Theory of Truth,* in *Philosophical Essays,* first published by Longmans, Green 1910. Reprinted by Allen and Unwin, 1966. |
| O.D. | 'On Denoting', *Mind* 1905, reprinted in *Logic and Knowledge.* |

O.KN.E.W.              *Our Knowledge of the External World,* first published by
                       The Open Court Publishing Co. 1914. Reprinted by
                       Allen and Unwin 1926.
O.N.A.                 'On the Nature of Acquaintance', *Monist* 1914,
                       reprinted in *Logic and Knowledge.*
O.N.T. and F.          'On the Nature of Truth and Falsehood', in
                       *Philosophical Essays.*
O.P.                   'On Propositions: What they are and how they mean',
                       *Proceedings of the Aristotelian Society Supplementary* Vol. II
                       1919, reprinted in *Logic and Knowledge.*
P.M.                   *Principia Mathematica Vol. I,* with A.N. Whitehead, first
                       published by Cambridge University Press 1910, 2nd
                       edition with a new introduction 1935.
P. of M.               *The Principles of Mathematics,* first published by the
                       Cambridge University Press 1903, 2nd edition with a
                       new Introduction 1937. Reprinted by Allen and Unwin
                       1950.
P. of PH.              *The Problems of Philosophy,* Oxford University Press, first
                       published 1912, 2nd edition 1967.
PH. of L.              *A Critical Exposition of the Philosophy of Leibniz,* first
                       published by the Cambridge University Press 1900.
                       Reprinted by Allen and Unwin 1937.
R. S–D. PH.            'The Relation of Sense-data to Physics', *Scientia* 1914,
                       reprinted in *Mysticism and Logic.*
R.U.P.                 'On the Relations of Universals and Particulars',
                       *Proceedings of the Aristotelian Society,* 1911-1912.
U.C.M.                 'The Ultimate Constituents of Matter', *Monist* 1915,
                       reprinted in *Mysticism and Logic.*


PART TWO *Other Authors*

Ayer, A. J.            *Russell and Moore: the Analytical Heritage,* Macmillan
                       1971.
Eames, E. R.           *Bertrand Russell's Theory of Knowledge,* Allen and Unwin
                       1969.
Klemke, E. D.          (Editor) *Essays on Bertrand Russell,* University of Illinois
                       Press 1970.
Pears, D. F.           *Bertrand Russell and the British Tradition in Philosophy,*
                       Fontana 1967, 2nd edition 1968.
Pears, D. F.           (Editor) *Bertrand Russell,* in the series *Modern Studies in
                       Philosophy* under the general editorship of A. Rotyr,
                       Doubleday 1972.
Schilpp, P. A.         *The Philosophy of Bertrand Russell,* Vol. V in *The Library of
                       Living Philosophers,* first published in 1944, latest edition
                       Harper and Row 1963.
Schoenman, R.          *Bertrand Russell: Philosopher of the Century,* Allen and
                       Unwin 1967.
Watling, J.            *Bertrand Russell,* Oliver and Boyd 1971.

# Chronological Tables

| | |
|---|---|
| 1872 | Born. |
| 1890–4 | Undergraduate at Trinity College, Cambridge. |
| 1894 | Married Alys Pearsall Smith (marriage dissolved 1921). |
| 1895 | Elected Fellow of Trinity College, Cambridge. |
| 1900 | Attended International Congress of Philosophy, Paris. |
| 1903 | *Principles of Mathematics* published. |
| 1908 | Elected Fellow of the Royal Society. |
| | Appointed Lecturer in the principles of mathematics, Trinity College, Cambridge. |
| 1910 | *Principia Mathematica Vol I* (with A. N. Whitehead) published. |
| 1912 | *Principia Mathematica Vol II* (with A. N. Whitehead) published. |
| | *The Problems of Philosophy* published. |
| | Met Wittgenstein. |
| 1913 | *Principia Mathematica Vol III* (with A. N. Whitehead) published. |
| 1914 | Visiting Professor, Harvard University: gave Lowell Lectures, published as *Our Knowledge of the External World as a Field for Scientific Method in Philosophy*. |
| 1916 | Fined £100 and deprived of his lectureship at Trinity College, Cambridge for writing a leaflet in defence of an imprisoned conscientious objector. |
| 1918 | Imprisoned for anti-war article. |
| 1919 | *Introduction to Mathematical Philosophy* and *Philosophy of Logical Atomism* published. |
| 1920 | Visited Russia. |
| 1920–1 | Visited China. |
| 1921 | Married Dora Black (marriage dissolved 1935). |
| | *The Analysis of Mind* published. |
| 1924 | *Logical Atomism* published. |
| 1927 | Founded progressive school with Dora Russell. |
| | *The Analysis of Matter* published. |
| 1928 | *Sceptical Essays* published. |
| 1929 | *Marriage and Morals* published. |
| 1931 | *The Scientific Outlook* published. |
| 1936 | Married Patricia Spence (marriage dissolved 1952). |
| 1938–44 | Lived in U.S.A. |
| 1940 | *An Inquiry Into Meaning and Truth* published. |
| 1944 | Appointed Lecturer at Trinity College, Cambridge. |
| | *My Mental Development* and *Reply to Criticism* appeared in *The* |

|  | *Philosophy of Bertrand Russell,* ed. P. A. Schilpp. |
| 1945 | *A History of Western Philosophy* published. |
| 1948 | *Human Knowledge: Its Scope and Limits* published. |
| 1949 | Gave Reith Lectures, 'Authority and the Individual'. |
| 1950 | Awarded Order of Merit. |
|  | Awarded Nobel Prize. |
| 1952 | Married Edith Finch. |
| 1954 | B.B.C. broadcast on nuclear warfare, 'Man's Peril'. |
| 1955 | Wrote manifesto, based on this broadcast, signed by Einstein and many other eminent scientists. |
| 1956 | Went to live in North Wales. |
| 1957 | Attended Pugwash Conference in Austria. |
|  | Helped to launch Campaign for Nuclear Disarmament. |
| 1959 | *My Philosophical Development* published. |
| 1960 | Supported civil disobedience and resigned from C.N.D. |
| 1961 | Imprisoned briefly for taking part in demonstration organized by committee of 100. |
| 1963 | Bertrand Russell Peace Foundation and Atlantic Peace Foundation set up. |
| 1965 | Resigned from Labour Party in protest against Government's Foreign Policy. |
| 1966 | First meeting of International War Crimes Tribunal. |
| 1967 | *War Crimes in Vietnam* published. |
|  | *The Autobiography of Bertrand Russell Vol I* published. |
| 1968 | *The Autobiography of Bertrand Russell Vol II* published. |
| 1969 | *The Autobiography of Bertrand Russell Vol III* published. |
|  | Died. |

# Index

*Index entries in bold type also appear in Part One of the Bibliography where references are given to other works by Russell in which these topics are discussed.*

187